Real World
Personal Finance

Real World Personal Finance

Mark A. Nadler and Terry E. Rumker

LEXINGTON BOOKS
Lanham • Boulder • New York • London

Published by Lexington Books
An imprint of The Rowman & Littlefield Publishing Group, Inc.
4501 Forbes Boulevard, Suite 200, Lanham, Maryland 20706
www.rowman.com

16 Carlisle Street, London W1D 3BT, United Kingdom

British Library Cataloguing in Publication Information Available

Library of Congress Cataloging-in-Publication Data

Nadler, Mark A.
  Real world personal finance / Mark A. Nadler and Terry E. Rumker.
      pages cm
  ISBN 978-0-7391-8876-7 (pbk. : alk. paper)—ISBN 978-0-7391-8877-4 (electronic)
1. Finance, Personal. 2. Investments. I. Rumker, Terry E. II. Title.
  HG179.N324 2014
  332.024—dc23

                                                                    2014013226

Printed in the United States of America

Contents

vi   *Contents*

To Instructors

The writing style in *Real World Personal Finance* is casual. We want to have a conversation with your students about personal finance. Throughout the book, we push, beg, and cajole readers to treat the financial side of their life seriously—that's our real purpose. If after reading and acting on our advice your students begin to act financially responsible then we've succeeded.

The pedagogy used in *Real World Personal Finance* is learning-by-doing. Because personal financial skills can't be acquired without applying them we have students practice personal finance throughout the book. Experiential learning is the key to changing behavior: Once your students engage in applying the book's material to their lives, questions and excitement will fill class time as opposed to note taking and clock watching.

When students complete *Real World Personal Finance*, they will have set financial goals adjusted for inflation, calculated their monthly costs, and built them into a budget. We also have students track their spending for a month, show them how to pay down debt, share with them tricks for increasing their FICO scores, and many other financial house cleaning chores necessary to become financially healthy.

Most books and courses on personal finance fail to change long-run behavior. The reason for this is simple: reading and listening to lectures on personal finance while helpful, don't change behavior. Americans know that they should eat properly, exercise, save, get out of debt, and so on; and still many don't act on this advice. For most of us, information by itself isn't motivating.

We front-load *Real World Personal Finance* with critical activities to engage students in the construction of their personal financial plan. This immediately excites them about personal finance. We then follow with subject content chapters they need to learn. Finally, we return to the integration of their financial goals into a balanced budget. A balanced budget that includes financial goals we call an *Action Plan*.

As students proceed, they fill out worksheets. Please collect and critically evaluate them. At the end of the book, students use these worksheets to construct their *Action Plan*. While we give our students formal tests, we give primary weight to student effort and the construction of their *Action Plan*. Ultimately, this is what we believe should determine their grade.

To Students

Personal finance is one of the most important subjects you'll study and if you act on the advice given in *Real World Personal Finance* it will, over your lifetime, not only pay for your education but make you wealthier by many thousands of dollars—not bad for a single course.

However, increased financial wealth is the not the most important thing you'll get from learning our materials and practicing our assignments. By becoming financially literate, you'll achieve greater financial security. Financially secure individuals live happier and less stressful lives. The world has become less stable. While young, it's important to lay the foundation for your financial wellness.

1

✛

Introduction
to Personal Finance

BOOK COVERAGE

The goal of *Real World Personal Finance* is to motivate and teach you to build a personal financial plan. This is not a mechanical process. You must also acquire some basic financial knowledge and the desire to make your plan a part of your life.

Chapter 2 introduces you to the personal financial problem. Here you'll see the link between saving, investing, and financial goals. Chapter 3 tortures you a bit with forcing you to learn something about the time value of money. The calculations you learn in this chapter are invaluable to your future success. Please study and learn them.

Chapter 4 is our busiest chapter. Here you'll set financial goals, adjust them for inflation, and calculate their cost. Don't be concerned by this chapter's workload. We'll help you through each step.

Chapter 5 is our dreaded tracking chapter. Tracking is a way of discovering where you spend your money. This is probably the book's most powerful exercise. Learning where you spend your money will change your life and allow you to control your outlays. Many people avoid tracking because of the effort it requires. Believe us, it's worth doing. This one exercise has changed the lives of millions of people.

Chapter 6 discusses the preparation stage for investing. This involves a certain amount of financial housecleaning: reducing or eliminating your credit card debt, creating an emergency fund, and reviewing your insurance needs.

Chapters 7 through 12 work at building your financial vocabulary. Investors have created a rich language to describe what they do. Chapters 13 through 15 cover the basics of personal investing with an emphasis on finding investment funds, understanding investment strategies, planning for retirement and college, and exploring tax shelters.

Chapter 16 integrates all of your previous work into an *action plan*. This plan is a budget that includes your financial goals. An *action plan* is your guide to financial wellness.

Chapters 17 discusses the college choice question including what majors currently have the highest pay outs and introduces you to the mess that's called federal student loans.

Chapters 18 through 21 explore reasons people fail to invest, how to purchase mutual funds, and how to select a financial planner.

Chapter 22 introduces you to the life-cycle element in investing. Personal finance for a twenty-five-year-old looks different than personal finance for a fifty-five-year-old. If you're twenty-five years old it's still important to begin thinking about the future personal finance choices you'll need to be making.

While reading this material, we'll direct you to chapter worksheets. Here you'll put into practice what you're learning. A big part of this effort involves learning about your existing spending patterns and calculating the savings necessary to reach each of your financial goals.

Advice 1

Spend time each week learning about personal finance beyond class assignments. An easy way to accomplish this is by watching financial news programs such as CNBC *and* Bloomberg TV *and reading the personal finance section of newspapers such as the* Wall Street Journal.

WHY YOU NEED TO PLAN YOUR FINANCIAL FUTURE

Americans used to feel financially secure about their future. Job security and seniority work rules, traditional employer pension plans, Social Security, and Medicare all worked together to guarantee a reasonable standard of living during working years and retirement. Corporate downsizing, outsourcing, foreign competition, the death of traditional pension plans, Social Security and Medicare possible running out of money, and now a weak economy and turbulent financial markets have made financial security as endangered as the white rhinoceros. Today, the only way for you to secure your future is through career and financial planning.

We're going to focus on financial planning and your need to save and invest for retirement and other financial goals such as being able to survive a bout of unemployment, having money for a down payment on a home and help paying for your children's education.

A seismic event that has occurred in the American workplace is the replacement of traditional pensions with various employer sponsored tax deferred savings plans like the 401(k) and 403(b), private tax deferred accounts like the IRA and Keogh, and the Roth IRA.

When working under a traditional pension plan, employers guarantee your retirement income. Here the cost of ignoring your retirement needs is modest. In a world of employer sponsored tax deferred savings plans you must determine both how much to save and how to invest your savings. In this circumstance, remaining financially illiterate means you'll be poor in the future.

People give many reasons why they fail to do financial planning. Here are just a few examples: "Heck, my retirement is still a million years away, I've got plenty of time to start saving." "Save money, are you crazy? I can hardly pay my current bills." Here's our favorite one, "Retire! Why bother? I'm probably going to be dead before I can spend a dime of my money!" While all of these are amusing, for individuals making these excuses a bleak financial future awaits them and this isn't funny.

Whenever we hear nonsense excuses, we pull out Terry's list of "What ifs" designed to send chills down your spine:

- What if the US economy nosedives and you lose your job, do you have sufficient cash reserves to pay your bills for six months or even a year?
- What if you become disabled and can't work, do you have sufficient disability insurance to pay your family's bills?
- What if your family's breadwinner passes away, do you have sufficient life insurance to make up the financial shortfall?
- What if your company declares bankruptcy and its traditional pension program goes kaput, where will you get money to retire?
- What if Social Security cuts benefits or extends the age of retirement, do you have sufficient savings to cover this highly likely event?
- What if in the year you plan to retire the stock market collapses, how will this affect your ability to retire?

- What if during retirement, financial markets "turn south" for three years, four years, or even five years, do you have sufficient wealth to live until it recovers?
- What if your son turns out not be a great quarterback and your daughter turns out not to be a genius, do you have sufficient savings to help pay for part of your children's education?
- What if you live much longer than you expected, do you have enough wealth to carry you an extra five or even ten years during retirement?
- What if inflation skyrockets and your favorite meal, a can of chicken noodle soup now costs ten dollars, do you have sufficient wealth to live through a major period of inflation?
- What if during retirement you're health fails, do you have sufficient savings to pay all of your uncovered medical bills?
- What if during the last part of your life you need intensive care, will you have the money to pay for it without leaving your partner or children financially impoverished?

Answers to these "What ifs" depend on your personal circumstances. What we know is that you should be thinking about and planning for these possibilities. *Real World Personal Finance* is designed to help you cope with unexpected events even if we don't specifically address each of them.

Fortunately, financial planning isn't only about avoiding some lurking disaster. There are good things in life that also require financial planning: education, weddings, down-payments on homes, vacations, and generous gifts. One we promote for young parents and even grandparents is to begin a million dollar savings plan for children and grandchildren. This isn't as impossible as it appears if it's begun at birth. With the knowledge you gain by reading and studying *Real World Personal Finance* you'll be able to start a millionaire program for all of your children.

2

✛

Understanding the Personal Financial Investment Problem

CONSUMPTION SAVINGS PROBLEM

Before you can invest money to cover your future needs you must learn to save. This is an obstacle for many Americans who just don't save enough money to cover their future consumption needs. After you pay your taxes and other deductions from your paycheck, you face a critical choice: how much of your disposable income will you spend now and how much will you save.

Review figure 2.1 below.

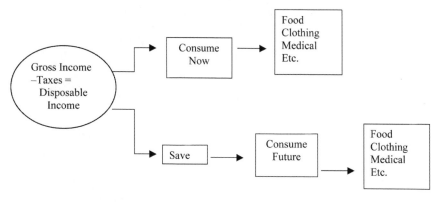

Figure 2.1. The Consumption Savings Problem.

What this flow diagram teaches us is to live today and plan for the future. Savings is just future consumption. The more you consume now the less you'll consume in the future. The less you consume now the more you'll consume in the future. It's really that easy.

Your goal should be to live a balanced life between the present and the future. Many of us choose to consume almost everything today. This is why Americans have one of the world's lowest savings rates. The key to maximizing your happiness is to live a balanced life across all of your life stages.

INVESTMENT PROBLEM

It's impossible to begin a rational program of saving and investing unless you understand the personal financial investment problem.

Look at figure 2.2 below.

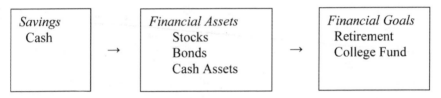

Figure 2.2.   The Investment Problem

It starts with savings in the form of cash. Three paper assets compete for your savings: stocks, bonds, and cash. Your financial goals are what you want to achieve in your savings and investment program. Taken together, this defines the problem of saving and investing. We state this problem as follows: How should you divide your savings between stocks, bonds, and cash assets such that you accomplish your financial goals quickly, inexpensively, and as risk-free as possible?

A well-defined financial goal states a money, income, or wealth target and a defined time frame. Here are some examples: "In ten years, I want to pay off all of my student loans." "In six years, when my eldest child reaches the age of eighteen, I want to give her $25,000 toward her college education." "In thirty-five years, I want $3,000,000 in wealth." It's easy to imagine other examples.

Once your financial goals are properly stated, they'll determine the types of assets you should invest and how much you must save. Take the example of a twenty-five-year-old who wants at age fifty, $500,000 in wealth. Presently, his net worth— net worth is the difference between what you own (i.e., assets) and what you owe (i.e., liabilities)—is zero. To accomplish this goal, he must ask and answer two questions. How much must I save each year and how should I allocate my savings between cash, bonds, and stocks to reach this goal. As you'll discover later, these two questions are connected.

Given this individual's goal is twenty-five years away, an investment strategy focused on stocks is probably appropriate. To simplify things, assume that this is the only asset invested in and stocks return 10 percent per year. This means that every dollar invested earns ten cents a year.

Next, is the savings question: How much must I save each year for the next twenty-five years to accumulate $500,000 in financial assets? If you assume an annual return of 10 percent, the answer is approximately $4,600. Later, we'll show you how to make this calculation.

This example also illustrates the power of compounding. If you multiply $4,600 by twenty-five (years), it equals $115,000. Where did the other $385,000 come from? Yes, compound earnings! This is money earned from receiving a return on returns.

Advice 2

Begin thinking about and writing down your final goals. Without them, it's impossible to develop a program of saving and investing.

3

✛

Calculating How Much Money You Need

What keeps many people from being able to do any financial planning is their inability to calculate what things will cost them in the future and how much they'll need to save to reach your financial goals. Making these calculations and understanding what they mean sounds difficult but we'll show you that they're easy and fun (if you're a financial weirdo) to do.

FUTURE VALUE CALCULATION

Let's start with a simple future value calculation. Today, you invest $100 in the stock market. Over the next five years this investment earns 6 percent annually. What will its future value be at the end of year five?

First, you have to understand what the 6 percent means. If on January 1 you make this $100 investment what will it be worth one year later on December 31? Take the $100 and multiply it by 1.06 (1 + 6 percent) and you have the answer. Correct, $106. Now let the $106 stay invested for one year at 6 percent. What will it be worth? Correct, take the $106 and multiply it by 1.06 and you get $112.36.

We could keep repeating the process of multiplying last year's investment by 1.06 and eventually answer our question of what a $100 investment returning 6 percent annually will be worth in five years. This procedure obviously is tedious and one we want to avoid.

One solution to this problem is to use what's called a future value table. Take a minute and turn to appendix 1. Review the content of this table.

Chapter 3

Below we've reproduced a part of this table. The table's columns tell you how fast something is growing. In the example we're working on our $100 is growing 6 percent a year. The table's rows tell you how many time periods we're allowing something to grow. So, again, in our example we're letting our $100 grow for five years or five time periods.

This table and the other table we want you to use assume a $1 investment. If you look at the cell that intersects column 6 percent and row 1 it equals 1.06. One way of interpreting this number is to think of it as $1.06. If you invest a $1 for one period and it's growing at .06 it will be worth $1.06 after one year.

How would you solve the problem we're working on? Correct. Go to column 6 percent and row 5. The number in the cell is 1.3382. What does this number mean? If you invested $1 for five years and it grew at 6 percent it would be worth $1.3382. However, you invested $100. To solve your problem you must multiply $100 by 1.3382. The correct answer is $133.82.

Table 3.1. Future Value of Present Sum

	Rates	1%	2%	3%	4%	5%	6%	7%
Periods								
1		1.0100	1.0200	1.0300	1.0400	1.0500	1.0600	1.0700
2		1.0201	1.0404	1.0609	1.0816	1.1025	1.1236	1.1449
3		1.0303	1.0612	1.0927	1.1249	1.1576	1.1910	1.2250
4		1.0406	1.0824	1.1255	1.1699	1.2155	1.2625	1.3108
5		1.0510	1.1041	1.1593	1.2167	1.2763	1.3382	1.4026
6		1.0615	1.1262	1.1941	1.2653	1.3401	1.4185	1.5007
7		1.0721	1.1487	1.2299	1.3159	1.4071	1.5036	1.6058
8		1.0829	1.1717	1.2668	1.3686	1.4775	1.5938	1.7182
9		1.0937	1.1951	1.3048	1.4233	1.5513	1.6895	1.8385
10		1.1046	1.2190	1.3439	1.4802	1.6289	1.7908	1.9672
11		1.1157	1.2434	1.3842	1.5395	1.7103	1.8983	2.1049
12		1.1268	1.2682	1.4258	1.6010	1.7959	2.0122	2.2522
13		1.1381	1.2936	1.4685	1.6651	1.8856	2.1329	2.4098

Mini table of future value of present sum rates 1–7 and periods.

In the problem we solved the $100 initial investment is called a present value while the $133.82 is its future value.

Try these two practice problems using appendix 1. Answers in appendix 4.

1. After working a couple of years your employer gives you a bonus of $2,500. After reading *Personal Finance for the Real World* you decide to invest this money for forty years (retirement). You expect to earn an 8 percent annual return. Calculate what it will be worth in forty years.
2. Your first child is born. Your parents give your child a $10,000 present. You decide to invest this money to help pay for her college education. The money will stay invested for eighteen years and you expect to earn 5 percent annually on this money. How much money will your child have after eighteen years?

FUTURE VALUE OF AN ANNUITY CALCULATION

Future value of an annuity calculation sounds complicated but it's not with the help of our table. Let's expand on our previous example of investing $100. Now let's assume that instead of investing a $100 once and waiting five years you invest $100 each year for five years. What will your $100 dollar yearly investment be worth in five years? To make this calculation you must consult an annuity table.

Go to appendix 2. This is an annuity table. Spend a moment reviewing it. Below is a slice of the table.

Table 3.2. Future Value of Annunity

	Rates	1%	2%	3%	4%	5%	6%	7%
Periods								
1		1.0000	1.0000	1.0000	1.0000	1.0000	1.0000	1.0000
2		2.0100	2.0200	2.0300	2.0400	2.0500	2.0600	2.0700
3		3.0301	3.0604	3.0909	3.1216	3.1525	3.1836	3.2149
4		4.0604	4.1216	4.1836	4.2465	4.3101	4.3746	4.4399
5		5.1010	5.2040	5.3091	5.4163	5.5256	5.6371	5.7507

Mini table future value of an annuity interest 1–7 and periods 1–5.

Again, let's begin with the 6 percent column. The cell located at the period 1/column 6 percent intersection is 1. You can treat this as $1. What does this mean? It means that on December 31 of year one you invested a dollar.

Now go to the cell located at the period 2/column 6 percent intersection. How would you interpret the 2.06? Again, you can treat it as $2.06. But what does it mean and how was it derived? The dollar you invested the previous year is now worth $1.06 ($1 x 1.06) and on December 31 of the second year you invested a second dollar. Together they equal $2.06.

Let's keep analyzing this table so that you understand it. The cell number at the intersection of period 3/column 6 percent is 3.1836. Treat it as $3.1836. Hold on because its explanation is going to be a bit lengthy. The dollar you initially invested grew into $1.06 during period two. That dollar now grows another 6 percent so that it is now worth $1.1236 ($1.06 x 1.06). The dollar you invested in period 2 is now worth $1.06 ($1 x 1.06). Plus you have the dollar you invest December 31 of period 3. Add all of these dollars together and you have $3.1836 ($1.1236 + $1.06 + $1).

If you're thoroughly confused then don't worry. We have a solution. Whenever you're making multiple equal investments and you want to know their future value then you can just use our annuity table. Returning to our example, if you invest $100 a year (remember, our table assumes that you invest this money on December 31 of any year) and expect to earn 6 percent annually then all you have to do is to multiply your $100 by the cell number located at the intersection of period 5 and column 6 percent. That number is 5.6371. Thus the answer is $100 x 5.6371 = $563.71

Try these two practice problems using appendix 2. Answers in appendix 4.

3. You and your partner want to begin a savings program for a down payment on a house. Together you decide to save $2,500 a year. You expect to earn 4 percent on your savings. How much will you have after five years?
4. You decide to save for your retirement. Your plan is to save $5,000 a year for fifty years. You assume that you'll earn 7 percent on your investments. How much will you have after fifty years?

PRESENT VALUE OF AN ANNUITY

Here's examples of types of questions you must be able to answer: In forty years, I want two million dollars (for retirement). In five years, I need $40,000 for a down payment on a house. In eighteen years, I need $50,000 to help pay for my child's college education.

All of these questions have a targeted amount and you need to calculate how much you must save yearly to reach the target. When we looked at the future value of an annuity you were asking if I invest some dollar amount per period, and I receive a certain percentage return each period, after some number of periods how much will I have? Now we're asking, I want some number of dollars in the future. Given some investment return, how much must I invest each period? This is what is meant by a present value annuity calculation.

Let's take our two million dollar target in forty years. Assume you believe that you can earn 10 percent annually. Go to appendix 2—yes, the future value of annuity table. You know the drill; go to column 10 percent and period 40. The number in the cell is 442.5926. To find the present value of an annuity divide your targeted dollar amount by the appropriate cell number. In this example, divide two million by 442.5926. The answer is $4,518.83. This means that if you save $4,518.83 each year for forty years, and you earn on average 10 percent return each year, you will end up with two million dollars. Pretty cool?

Practice by doing the two questions we asked earlier.

CALCULATORS

The way all of these questions are answered in the real world is with calculators. We supply and use tables in *Real World Personal Finance* because we assume that you don't have immediate access to calculators while working your way through our material.

A great web site, packed with all kinds of financial calculators, is www.dinkytown.net. *Go play.*

4

Financial Goal Setting

Roll-up your sleeves because you're about to do some of the most important work of your life: setting financial goals, adjusting them for inflation and calculating their costs. Let's begin with goal setting.

LIST YOUR FINANCIAL GOALS

Setting financial goals is the first step in personal financial planning. Until you know where you want to go it's impossible to get anywhere. This is what we want you to do now.

The worksheets that follow structure your financial goals by length of time and dollar amounts. For each period, we list appropriate types of financial assets.

Financial goals fall into three timeframes: short-term, medium-term, and long-term. We suggest lengths of time for each; feel free to modify these a bit if you want. For each timeframe, list your financial goals. Try to be as specific as possible about listing required dollar amounts. Set these goals with your spouse or partner.

Include only your most important financial goals. Don't include everyday living expense items like paying for groceries, rent, or gas.

If you have credit card debt and student loans make sure to include them.

Each financial goal listed should include its purpose, dollar amount, and timeframe.

Short-Term Goals: One to Two Years Away

Appropriate types of financial assets: cash assets such as bank accounts, CDs, and online savings accounts.

Examples: payoff credit cards and other forms of debt, vacations, Christmas presents.

Table 4.1. Short-term Financial Goals.

Short-Term Financial Goals		
Purpose	Current Dollar Amount	Years to Goal
Payoff credit card debt	$3000	2

Medium-Term Goals: Three to Seven Years Away

Appropriate types of financial assets: CDs, short- and medium-term bonds and bond funds, balanced mutual funds, and blue chip stock mutual funds.

Examples: build emergency fund, payoff student loans, save for house down-payment.

Long-Term Goals: Greater Than Seven Years Away

Appropriate types of financial assets: bond funds, growth and income funds, stock mutual funds, growth stock mutual funds, and international stock mutual funds.

Examples: retirement planning, payoff student loans, college planning for children, starting your children on a lifetime savings program.

Table 4.2. **Medium-term Financial Goals.**

Medium-Term Financial Goals		
Purpose	Current Dollar Amount	Years to Goal
Build Emergency fund	$10,000	5

Table 4.3. **Long-term Financial Goals.**

Long-Term Financial Goals		
Purpose	Current Dollar Amount	Years to Goal
Retirement	$2,000,000	40

BUILD INFLATION INTO YOUR GOALS

Inflation is a rise in prices overtime. In the twentieth century, prices rose on average by 3 percent. This translates into a doubling of prices about every twenty-four years or the halving of the value of your money. Financial goals, whose real cost is not fixed, must be adjusted for inflation. (Don't be fooled by the lack of inflation today. Even an inflation rate of one or two percent has a large effect on the value of your money over decades.)

This worksheet explains how to build inflation into your final goals. Return to your list of financial goals with their dollar amounts. The dollar amounts listed need an inflation adjustment by multiplying them by an inflation multiplier to arrive at their future cost.

For example, in forty years you want to save $2,000,000 for retirement. The problem is that a dollar forty years from today will not be worth a dollar today assuming an inflation rate of 3 percent. In fact, it will be worth just around thirty-one cents. You must account for this depreciation (lowering) of the value of money when setting the true cost of your goals. In the example of a $2,000,000 retirement goal, you need to save $6,524,000 dollars in forty years to have the equivalent of $2,000,000 in today's purchasing power.

We understand that these adjustments can be discouraging. However, there is no point hiding from reality. Also, keep in mind that your salary will also increase overtime so that these goals, which appear unreachable, will be less overwhelming than they now appear.

Let's return to our retirement calculation and see how we did it. Go to appendix 1 titled "Future Value of Present Sum." Go to the 3 percent column and row 40. The number that appears in the cell is 3.2620. In this example, we call this number an inflation multiplier. We then multiplied $2,000,000 by this number to come up with $6,524,000.

For many of your goals assume an inflation rate of at least 3 percent. Some goals, like saving for your child's education, require a higher rate such as 5 percent. For each goal, you must figure out its appropriate inflation multiplier. If in doubt, using 3 percent will cover many real world goals.

Caution

Some goals, like paying off credit card debt, require a different calculation. If you are trying to pay off a loan or credit card balance, interest on these loans is calculated differently and requires the use of a loan or credit card calculator.

Assume you have $2,000 in credit card debt and pay an annual rate of 17.50 percent. Go to www.dinkytown.com and locate their "Credit Cards and Debt Calculators." Select the calculator called Credit Card Payoff. Enter $2,000, 17.50 percent, and assume you want to pay it off in twenty-four months. Enter what you currently pay (assume $125) and your additional monthly charges (assume $100) and your annual fee (assume $35). Click on "Calculate" button. You new payment comes to $204 a month or an additional $79 over what you currently pay.

To repay federal student loans go to: www2.ed.gov/offices/OSFAP/ DirectLoan/RepayCalc/dlentry1.html.

You will be asked to state your outstanding loans, outstanding *principal* (what you owe) and interest, and who your *loan servicer* is. You will need your Federal Student Aid PIN to sign in to the National Student Loan Data System. Separate calculators also exist for Income-Contingent Repayment Plan (ICR) calculator and Income-Based Repayment Plan (IBR) Calculator.

Both ICR and IBR are intended to provide you with an affordable monthly payment amount. Under both plans, any remaining loan balance is forgiven after twenty-five years, and payments made can count toward the 120 payments required for Public Service Loan Forgiveness. In general, IBR is the better choice for most borrowers. However, everyone's situation is unique and you must further investigate your options under both plans.

At the end of this chapter, we provide you with a worksheet to list all of your outstanding debt and the cost of paying it off.

PROCEDURE FOR ADJUSTING
FINANCIAL GOALS FOR INFLATION

Below are the steps for adjusting a financial goal for inflation.

Step 1: Current cost of future goal $ _____
Step 2: Assumed inflation rate _____ Years to final goal _____
Step 3: Appropriate multiplier _____
Step 4: (Step 1 amount $ _____) (×) (Step 3 amount _____) =
Future cost of goal $ _____

Let's work through another example using the above format. Say that in four years you want to purchase a car that's currently selling for $20,000. You believe that new car prices are rising at 4 percent a year. What will its selling price be in four years?

Step 1: Current cost of future goal $20,000
Step 2: Assumed inflation rate 4%, Years to final goal 4 years
Step 3: Appropriate multiplier 1.1699 (Appendix 1, 4% column, 4th row)
Step 4: (Step 1 amount $20,000) (×) (Step 3 amount 1.1699) = $23,398

This means the car that today costs $20,000 will cost you $23,398 in four years.

The only trick in this calculation is how to use appendix 1. Appendix 1 projects current values into the future assuming some growth rate. Columns in this appendix list growth rates and rows time periods. In this example, car prices are growing at 4 percent and the problem's time period is four years. Going to the spreadsheet's 4 percent column and row 4 the cell number 1.1699. Multiplying this number by $20,000 gives you the answer.

CALCULATIONS (IGNORE DEBT YOU WANT TO PAYOFF)

While the thrust of this work is to build inflation into your planning, any rising price trend can use this procedure. Now build inflation into each of your goals.

We list five goals under each time period. You don't have to have five goals per time period.

Short-Term Goals

Goal 1:

    Step 1: Current cost of future goal $ _____
    Step 2: Assumed inflation rate _____ , Years to final goal _____
    Step 3: Appropriate multiplier _____
    Step 4: (Step 1 amount _____) (×) (Step 3 amount _____)
    Future cost of future goal $ _____

Goal 2:

    Step 1: Current cost of future goal $ _____
    Step 2: Assumed inflation rate _____, Years to final goal _____
    Step 3: Appropriate multiplier _____
    Step 4: (Step 1 amount _____) (×) (Step 3 amount _____)
    Future cost of future goal $ _____

Goal 3:

    Step 1: Current cost of future goal $ _____
    Step 2: Assumed inflation rate _____, Years to final goal _____
    Step 3: Appropriate multiplier _____
    Step 4: (Step 1 amount _____) (×) (Step 3 amount _____)
    Future cost of future goal $ _____

Goal 4:

Step 1: Current cost of future goal $ _____
Step 2: Assumed inflation rate _____, Years to final goal _____
Step 3: Appropriate multiplier _____
Step 4: (Step 1 amount _____) (×) (Step 3 amount _____)

Goal 5:

Step 1: Current cost of future goal $ _____
Step 2: Assumed inflation rate _____, Years to final goal _____
Step 3: Appropriate multiplier _____
Step 4: (Step 1 amount _____) (×) (Step 3 amount _____)
Future cost of future goal $ _____

Medium-Term Goals

Goal 1:

Step 1: Current cost of future goal $ _____
Step 2: Assumed inflation rate _____, Years to final goal _____
Step 3: Appropriate multiplier _____
Step 4: (Step 1 amount _____) (×) (Step 3 amount _____)
Future cost of future goal $ _____

Goal 2:

Step 1: Current cost of future goal $ _____
Step 2: Assumed inflation rate _____, Years to final goal _____
Step 3: Appropriate multiplier _____
Step 4: (Step 1 amount _____) (×) (Step 3 amount _____)
Future cost of future goal $_____

Goal 3:

Step 1: Current cost of future goal $ _____
Step 2: Assumed inflation rate _____, Years to final goal _____
Step 3: Appropriate multiplier _____
Step 4: (Step 1 amount _____) (×) (Step 3 amount _____)
Future cost of future goal $ _____

Goal 4:

Step 1: Current cost of future goal $ _____
Step 2: Assumed inflation rate _____, Years to final goal _____

Step 3: Appropriate multiplier _____
Step 4: (Step 1 amount _____) (×) (Step 3 amount _____)
Future cost of future goal $ _____

Goal 5:

Step 1: Current cost of future goal $ _____
Step 2: Assumed inflation rate _____, Years to final goal _____
Step 3: Appropriate multiplier _____
Step 4: (Step 1 amount _____) (×) (Step 3 amount _____)
Future cost of future goal $ _____

Long-Term Goals

Goal 1:

Step 1: Current cost of future goal $ _____
Step 2: Assumed inflation rate _____, Years to final goal _____
Step 3: Appropriate multiplier _____
Step 4: (Step 1 amount _____) (×) (Step 3 amount _____)
Future cost of future goal $ _____

Goal 2:

Step 1: Current cost of future goal $ _____
Step 2: Assumed inflation rate _____, Years to final goal _____
Step 3: Appropriate multiplier _____
Step 4: (Step 1 amount _____) (×) (Step 3 amount _____)
Future cost of future goal $ _____

Goal 3:

Step 1: Current cost of future goal $ _____
Step 2: Assumed inflation rate _____, Years to final goal _____
Step 3: Appropriate multiplier _____
Step 4: (Step 1 amount _____) (×) (Step 3 amount _____)
Future cost of future goal $ _____

Goal 4:

Step 1: Current cost of future goal $ _____
Step 2: Assumed inflation rate _____, Years to final goal _____

Step 3: Appropriate multiplier _____
Step 4: (Step 1 amount _____) (×) (Step 3 amount _____)
Future cost of future goal $ _____

Goal 5:

Step 1: Current cost of future goal $ _____
Step 2: Assumed inflation rate _____, Years to final goal _____
Step 3: Appropriate multiplier _____
Step 4: (Step 1 amount _____) (×) (Step 3 amount _____)
Future cost of future goal $ _____

Some Key Points to Consider

- Since World War II, prices have risen continuously in the U.S.
- Some price increases are general in nature; others are unique to particular goods and services, such as education.
- Inflation reduces the purchasing power of money.
- Assume that prices will rise by at least 3 percent a year.
- Always build inflation into your financial calculations.

CALCULATING THE YEARLY SAVINGS REQUIREMENT FOR A FINANCIAL GOAL

Calculating a savings program to reach a financial goal is a three-step process. First, determine the future cost of your goal. This partly requires accounting for inflation and cost trends. You accomplished this in the previous section.

Second, assume a rate of return on the investments selected to reach each goal. You'll do this next. Finally, using the annuity table in appendix 2, you'll calculate the yearly savings necessary to reach each of your goals.

Because each of you face unique tax situations, we ignore taxes in our analysis. In fact, it's not difficult to build a tax rate into your savings calculations. We'll point out how to do it in a few places.

The Future Cost of Goals

Next we want you to move your future cost calculations to the summary statements below. Again, ignore your debt calculations. Later we build your debt repayment plan into an overall summary sheet.

Cost Short-Term Goals

Goal 1: Future Cost $ _____
Goal 2: Future Cost $ _____
Goal 3: Future Cost $ _____
Goal 4: Future Cost $ _____
Goal 5: Future Cost $ _____

Cost Medium-Term Goals:

Goal 1: Future Cost $ _____
Goal 2: Future Cost $ _____
Goal 3: Future Cost $ _____
Goal 4: Future Cost $ _____
Goal 5: Future Cost $ _____

Cost Long-Term Goals:

Goal 1: Future Cost $ _____
Goal 2: Future Cost $ _____
Goal 3: Future Cost $ _____
Goal 4: Future Cost $ _____
Goal 5: Future Cost $ _____

Determining Rates of Return

Inspect our list of suggested assets for each timeframe. Expand this list to include other appropriate types of assets you want to consider. You have to assume a rate of return for each cluster of assets selected to accomplish each goal. These rates of return are going to be different based on the length of time it takes to reach each goal.

There are no fixed rules in making these calculations but we strongly suggest making conservative estimates. For example, 7 percent return on your long-term goals, 5 percent on your medium-term goals, and 3 percent on your short-term goals. Current market conditions and your tolerance for risk will impact these returns.

Short-term goals:

Goal 1: Assumed rate of return _____%
Goal 2: Assumed rate of return _____%
Goal 3: Assumed rate of return _____%
Goal 4: Assumed rate of return _____%
Goal 5: Assumed rate of return _____%

Medium-term goals:

Goal 1: Assumed rate of return _____%
Goal 2: Assumed rate of return _____%
Goal 3: Assumed rate of return _____%
Goal 4: Assumed rate of return _____%
Goal 5: Assumed rate of return _____%

Long-term goals:

Goal 1: Assumed rate of return _____%
Goal 2: Assumed rate of return _____%
Goal 3: Assumed rate of return _____%
Goal 4: Assumed rate of return _____%
Goal 5: Assumed rate of return _____%

Calculating Your Yearly Savings Requirement for Each Goal

Go to appendix 2. This is the "Future Value of an Annuity" table. The column headings list rates of returns while the row headings list time-periods. This table tells you the future value of saving a dollar per period assuming some rate of return and time period. Appendix 2 assumes that a dollar is saved on December 31.

As an illustration, look at the 4 percent column. This column gives the answer to the following question: Assuming a rate of return of 4 percent per period, if you save a dollar each period, how many dollars will you have after some number of periods? For example, saving a dollar per year, how many dollars will you have after five years assuming a rate of return of 4 percent? The number in the cell is 5.4163. Multiply this by $1 and you get your answer, $5.42.

Another way of using this table is to find the amount you must save per period to reach some future dollar amount. Let's study the case of a couple, who, after much prodding from friends and family, develop a savings plan to buy the boat of their dreams. They want to save enough so that in five years they can purchase it. They estimate its future cost to be $22,000 and, being conservative, they assume a rate of return of 5 percent. How much must they save yearly to accumulate $22,000?

Go to appendix 2. Look down the column labeled 5 percent to row 5. The listed number is 5.5256. For this type of problem we call this a discount factor. Divide $22,000 by 5.5256. Rounded-off, it equals $3,981. This is the dollar amount they must save yearly for five years to accumulate $22,000.

In the above illustration, we ignored taxes. Returns on investments are taxed unless they're sheltered. One convenient way of reflecting taxes in your calculation is by reducing your assumed rate of return by your tax rate. For example, if our couple is in the 20 percent tax bracket—this means that out of every dollar they earn they must pay $0.20 in taxes—their effective rate of return equals 4 percent, not 5 percent. (If you earn 5 percent on your money and 20 percent of this amount is taxed then you have an effective rate of 4 percent. Twenty percent of 5 percent is 1 percent. Subtract this 1 percent from the 5 percent and you are left with 4 percent.) This would be the appropriate return for them to use in their calculation.

If you now go to the 4 percent column and row 5 in appendix 2 the discount factor is 5.3091. Dividing $22,000 by this number gives you a required yearly savings of $4,144. This couple must save more to offset taxes they must pay on their investment earnings.

Let's review this procedure. You have a future dollar amount you want to save. You know how many years you want to save to reach this target. You have assumed some yearly rate of return you expect to earn. With this information, go to appendix 2. Find the column with the rate of return you're assuming. Go down this column until you reach the number of time periods you're assuming. The number you see we call the discount factor. If you divide your targeted dollar amount by this discount factor, you'll have the yearly savings necessary to reach your goal—ignoring taxes.

Now do this for each of your goals except debt you want to pay off.

Short-Term Savings:

Goal 1: Future Cost of Financial Goal $ _____
        ÷ Discount Factor _____ = Yearly Savings Amount _____
Goal 2: Future Cost of Financial Goal $_____
        ÷ Discount Factor _____ = Yearly Savings Amount _____
Goal 3: Future Cost of Financial Goal $_____
        ÷ Discount Factor _____ = Yearly Savings Amount _____
Goal 4: Future Cost of Financial Goal $ _____
        ÷ Discount Factor _____ = Yearly Savings Amount _____
Goal 5: Future Cost of Financial Goal $ _____
        ÷ Discount Factor _____ = Yearly Savings Amount _____
Total _____

Medium-Term Savings

Goal 1: Future Cost of Financial Goal $_____
        ÷ Discount Factor _____ = Yearly Savings Amount _____
Goal 2: Future Cost of Financial Goal $_____
        ÷ Discount Factor _____ = Yearly Savings Amount _____

Goal 3: Future Cost of Financial Goal $_____
    ÷ Discount Factor _____ = Yearly Savings Amount _____
Goal 4: Future Cost of Financial Goal $ _____
    ÷ Discount Factor _____ = Yearly Savings Amount _____
Goal 5: Future Cost of Financial Goal $ _____
    ÷ Discount Factor _____ = Yearly Savings Amount _____
Total _____

Long-Term Savings:

Goal 1: Future Cost of Financial Goal $_____
    ÷ Discount Factor _____ = Yearly Savings Amount _____
Goal 2: Future Cost of Financial Goal $_____
    ÷ Discount Factor _____ = Yearly Savings Amount _____
Goal 3: Future Cost of Financial Goal $_____
    ÷ Discount Factor _____ = Yearly Savings Amount _____
Goal 4: Future Cost of Financial Goal $ _____
    ÷ Discount Factor _____ = Yearly Savings Amount _____
Goal 5: Future Cost of Financial Goal $ _____
    ÷ Discount Factor _____ = Yearly Savings Amount _____
Total _____

PAYING OFF DEBT

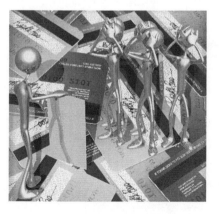

We strongly advise you to payoff credit card debt as quickly as you can. School related debt and all other forms of debt must also be built into your financial plans.

To make calculations related to credit card debt, go to www.dinky-town.com. Under "Credit Cards and Debt Calculator" select one of the credit card payoff calculators at this site. For school debt, go to www2. ed.gov/offices/OSFAP/Direct-Loan/RepayCalc/dlentry1.html.

To use any of these tools you must know the interest rate you are paying, your total debt burden, any annual fees you are being charged, and a payoff schedule.

Debt Pay Off Table

Complete this worksheet. At the very least, list all of your credit card debt. Use online calculators to fill out the "Monthly Payment" column.

Table 4.4. Pay Off Debt.

Dollar Amount Owed	Interest Charge (APR)	Annual Fees	Payoff Period	Monthly Payment
Total Monthly Payments				

Total Planned Savings and Debt Repayment Costs

Now add all of your savings costs and debt repayment costs together, and record the numbers below.

Total Yearly Savings Costs: $_____
Total Yearly Debt Repayment Costs: $_____
Total $_____

The budget we want you to calculate is on a monthly basis. To calculate your monthly savings and debt repayment divide your total by 12. The answer will be the amount you will need to save each month in order to reach all of your planned goals. This is a rough number because your required savings was calculated on a yearly basis. However, it will give you a sense of the cost of your savings plan.

Total ÷ 12 = $_____ (Monthly savings and debt repayment)

Can you afford this amount each month? Many people discover that they can't. Later we'll discuss strategies for dealing with this problem.

SUMMARY SHEET

This is the ultimate nerd table (table 4.5). We recommend you fill it out. It's very useful to summarize all of your calculations in one place. Being able to quickly review your goal information will allow you to make smarter decisions.

We entered a few examples in the summary sheet for you to follow. The summary sheet is broken into three sections: short-term, medium-term, and long-term goals. In the short-term section, we entered a goal of paying off credit card debt of $4,000 in two years. This example assumes you are paying 17.5 percent interest with no annual fee. Remember, to make calculations to pay down credit card debt you must use a calculator. In this example, we entered data for the first three columns and the last column. Those are the only places you need to enter information concerning debt repayment.

Under medium-term goals, we entered the goal of saving $50,000 for a house down payment. Assuming an inflation rate of 3 percent we then went to the 3 percent column, row 5, in appendix 1. The number listed in the cell is 1.193. We call this an inflation factor. Multiplying $50,000 by 1.193 gives us $57.965. This is the amount of down payment money we will need in five years assuming an inflation rate of 3 percent.

We then assumed a return on our savings of 5 percent. Going to appendix 2, column 5 percent and row 5, the number in the cell is 5.5256—the discount factor. Dividing $57,965 by 5.5256 gives you $10,490. Dividing $10,490 by 12 equals a monthly payment of $874.

Table 4.5. Goals Summary Table.

Goal	Time	Cost in Today's Dollars	Inflation Rate	Inflation Factor	Inflated Cost	Assumed Return	Annuity Factor	Annual Savings	Monthly Savings
C1	C2	C3	C4	C5	C6	C7	C8	C9	C10
Short-term				**Appendix 1**	**C3 x C5**		**Appendix 2**	**C6 ÷ C8**	**C9 ÷ 12**
Credit Card Debt	2 yrs	$4000							$199
Medium-term								**Total**	
House Down Payment	5 yrs	$50,000	3%	1.1593	$57,965	5%	5.5256	$10,490	$874
Long-term								**Total**	
								Total	
								Grand Total	

5

+

Track Your Spending

Now that you have set financial goals and calculated their costs, you have to determine whether you can afford them. The most powerful exercise to determine your current financial situation is learning how you spend your money. The average person has no idea where their money is spent. It's not uncommon for people to spend more than what they earn. You want to avoid becoming a negative saver.

Track your spending through chapter 15—in fact, you should track your spending the rest of your life. This is the only way to learn where your money is going. Later, when you put together your *Action Plan*—an *Action Plan* is a budget that contains your financial goals—you'll probably discover that not only can't you afford your financial goals but that you're probably spending more than you take in. The only way to figure out how to make room for your financial goals and get your budget into balance is by cutting back some of your expenditures. This requires that you know where you money is spent.

Tracking your spending is a tedious exercise. We don't want to lie to you and tell you it's either fun or easy to do—it's not. However, we have found that tracking spending is an eye-opening exercise for most people and usually leads to a more productive spending pattern.

RECORD EXPENSES FOR ONE MONTH

How much do you spend each month? Where does your money go? Most people can't answer both of these questions. This exercise will show you how much you spend and where it's spent.

Before proceeding to our worksheets, we want you to know that there are phone apps that make tracking your expenses very easy. We do not

Table 5.1.   Monthly Fixed Expense.

Monthly Fixed Expenses			
Date:			
Expense Categories	Actual Expenses	Budget Expenses	Savings
Mortgage/Rent			
Property Taxes			
Electricity			
Natural Gas			
Water			
Garbage Disposal			
Other:			
Total Fixed Home Costs			
Car Loan 1			
Car Loan 2			
Credit Card 1			
Credit Card 2			
Student Loans			
Other:			
Other:			
Total Loan Costs			
Alimony & Child Support			
Current Savings (401k, 403b, etc.)			
Home Insurance			
Car Insurance			
Health Insurance			
Life Insurance			
Disability Insurance			
Total Insurance Costs			
Total Fixed Cost			

want to recommend any particular app, but we do encourage you to investigate this option.

First, we want you to record your fixed costs in the "Monthly Fixed Expenses" work sheets. Fixed costs are expenses you can't change immediately such as a home mortgage payment or rent, a car payment, and a minimum credit card payment. Some of these occur monthly, such as your car payment. Others you pay quarterly, such as insurance. For fixed costs that are not monthly, calculate their average monthly cost by dividing them by twelve.

Under "Current Savings," record all savings that are part of a work-related retirement program. Even though you can change what you contribute, we want you to treat it as a fixed expense.

All tracking work sheets have three columns to record expenses: "Actual Expenses," "Budgeted Expenses," and "Amount Saved." For now, only enter expenses in the "Actual Expenses" column. Later, you'll enter "Budgeted Expenses" and "Amount Saved."

VARIABLE EXPENSES

Variable expenses are expenditures you can change quickly. Variable expenses that are billed monthly (e.g., phone, electricity, water) or paid by check and credit card are easy to track. Expenses paid out-of-pocket tend to be out-of-mind. We want you to also track this "wallet money" by recording outlays as they occur. This means walking around with a small notebook and recording each of your outlays. For example, if in the morning you leave home with $25, record during the day how you spend this money. Yes, we mean every nickel and dime! You'll be surprised how nickels and dimes add up over the course of a year.

Go now to the "Monthly Variable Expenses" work sheets. For now, we only want you to fill-in the "Actual Expenses" column. Later, you'll enter "Budgeted Expenses" and "Amount Saved."

While you're tracking we want to proceed and teach you the basic vocabulary and knowledge necessary to become financially secure. Later we'll return to this tracking exercise and use the knowledge you've gained to build an *Action Plan*.

Table 5.2. Monthly Variable Expenses

Monthly Variable Expenses			
Date:			
Expense Categories	Actual Expenses	Budget Expenses	Savings
Gasoline			
Car Repair			
Public Transportation			
Tolls/Parking Expenses			
License Fees			
Other:			
Total Transportation Costs			
Groceries			
Eating Meals Out			
Outside Snacks			
Children's Lunch Money			
Other:			
Total Food Costs			
Work Clothing (include footwear)			
Casual Clothing (include footwear)			
Children's Clothing (include footwear)			
Dry Cleaning			
Other:			
Total Clothing Costs			
School Tuition			
School Room and Board			
School Supplies			
Books			
School Activity Fees			
Professional/Association Memberships			
Newspaper/Magazine Subscriptions			
Other:			
Total Education Costs			
Cosmetics			
Hair Care (e.g. shampoo)			

Monthly Variable Expenses			
Date:			
Expense Categories	Actual Expenses	Budget Expenses	Savings
Sundries (e.g. soap, toothpaste, etc.)			
Other:			
Total Personal Care Costs			
Home Repair			
Yard Maintenance			
Furnishing			
Home Improvements			
Other:			
Total Home Costs			
Movies			
Vacations			
Weekend Trips			
Cable TV			
Internet			
Liquor/Wine			
Hobbies			
Health club/Country club			
Other:			
Total Entertainment Costs			
Out-of-Pocket Doctor Costs			
Out-of-Pocket Medicine Costs			
Out-of-Pocket Dental Costs			
Out-of-Pocket Hospital Costs			
Other:			
Total Health Costs			
Cell Phone(s)			
Tobacco			
Gifts			
Day Care			

Monthly Variable Expenses			
Date:			
Expense Categories	Actual Expenses	Budget Expenses	Savings
Pet Food			
Pet Vet Bills			
Children Allowances			
Other:			
Total Miscellaneous Costs			
Total Variable Costs (Add all variable cost work sheets)			

6

Pre-Investment Steps

Now that you've set your financial goals and have begun to track your spending, the next step you must take is to get your financial house in order. This requires a five-step process that we describe in this chapter.

One of the first things that financial planners do when they begin work with a new client is to assess their current situation. This includes a review of their assets and liabilities, emergency fund, insurance needs, mortgage, projected Social Security benefits, and the dollar amounts owed on their credit cards.

Before investing in financial assets (stocks, bonds, money market instruments), you should first consider doing the following:

- Establish an emergency fund
- Cover all insurance needs
- Purchase a home or explain why you're renting
- Check your Social Security benefits
- Pay off credit card debt

ESTABLISHING AN EMERGENCY FUND

Common advice is to establish an emergency fund before investing. This fund should be available for unexpected expenses, illness, et cetera. It should equal six to twelve months of your living expenses depending on the types of insurance policies you have, the nature of your work, your available credit lines, your age, and so forth. Job security and the availability of employment are the most important things to consider when deciding on how many months of living expenses to set aside.

We know married couples where each received termination notices from their respective employers within a two-week period. What would you do if that happened to you? How long could you pay your bills before your money ran out? Most Americans live paycheck to paycheck and would have to stop paying bills if one person lost their job let alone both. The only way to avoid this problem is to build an emergency fund.

Bank accounts that pay interest (savings, NOW accounts) or online savings accounts are excellent places to invest emergency money. These provide immediate access to your money and, unlike CDs, there is no penalty for early withdrawal. Another option is Series I Saving Bonds. The largest pluses for this instrument are its inflation protection and absolute security. Some downsides to Series I Saving Bonds is that they must be held for twelve months before cashing them in and if they are cashed in within five years there is a slight interest penalty.

COVERING INSURANCE NEEDS

Types of Insurance

The primary types of insurance are home, car, health, life, and disability. The purpose of insurance is to pay you for incurred losses on your home or apartment, compensate you for medical bills, pay your beneficiary upon your death, and pay you if you can't work because of a disability.

One complicating factor for certain types of insurance coverage, like home and car, is how your insurance company calculates the amount it will pay you for a loss. Two options exist: replacement and actual cash value. Replacement means that your insurance company will pay you an amount to replace the object damaged or if your model doesn't exist anymore of a like kind. Actual cash value means that your insurance company will pay you the object's market value—what the object is worth if you went to sell it.

Obviously, from your perspective replacement is normally better than actual market value—especially for objects that depreciate (i.e., lose value overtime). Insurance companies like actual cash value because their pay-out is normally less. Remember, if your insurance company gives you a choice and you select replacement value your insurance cost will be greater.

One decision you have to make for any type of insurance is how much of it do you want? While full coverage is always an option, sometimes it's smarter to buy partial coverage and use your insurance policy as a safety net to avoid bankruptcy. This is one way to save money on your insurance costs.

Home Owner's Insurance

The purpose of homeowner's insurance is to protect your home and its contents from damage and theft. Everyone needs home insurance and mortgage lenders require it.

Traditional home insurance is at your house's actual or market value assuming that you adjust your coverage as your home's value increases. With replacement insurance, you're paid an amount sufficient to rebuild your existing home no matter what its cost.

We recommend replacement insurance. This is the preferred type of coverage if you plan to stay in your home for greater than five years. This type of insurance is more costly but it will give you peace of mind if something should ever happen.

Home Insurance Example

Bob and Mary carry a $250,000 traditional (actual value) home insurance policy and a fire destroys their home. Bob and Mary receive $250,000. They then discover that to rebuild their house it will cost $300,000. Bob and Mary will be out $50,000 or they will have to build a smaller home. If they had purchased replacement insurance, it would have covered the $300,000 cost of rebuilding their home.

In addition, check if your home is covered for natural disasters like floods or water damage from drains backing up in your basement. Depending on where you live natural disaster coverage can be expensive but might be something you must have.

There is more to home insurance than the loss of your house. You also need to consider the content portion of your homeowner's policy. Many people ignore the replacement value of their jewelry, art, guns, computers, et cetera. Insurance companies pay very little for loss or damage to these items unless you pay extra to cover them.

Scheduled personal property is items you own that are worth more than what your policy will cover. If these objects are worth more than your policy limit, appraise them for their true value and have a schedule written for additional coverage. There will be an extra charge to have this added coverage.

Calculating Your Home Insurance Needs

Home coverage should be set at its replacement cost. This way you will have the money to rebuild it if it's destroyed.

This is basic home insurance information you should calculate.

Existing Home Coverage	$ _____	Home Value	$ _____
Home Replacement Cost	$ _____		
Content Coverage	$ _____	Content Value	$ _____
Deductible	$ _____		
Medical	$ _____		
Liability	$ _____		

Scheduled items (at replacement value).

Furs	$ _____
Jewelry	$ _____
Coins	$ _____

Collectibles: antiques, art.

Baseball Cards, etc.	$ _____
Computer Equipment	$ _____
Camera Equipment	$ _____
Boats	$ _____
Camper/RV	$ _____

Other Coverage.

Flood and Earthquake	$ _____

Total Cost of All Scheduled.

Items	$ _____

Auto Insurance

Anyone who drives a car is required to have insurance coverage or in some states, a posted bond. Some of the key terms for car insurance are premium, deductible, bodily injury liability, comprehensive, collision, and maximum payout.

"Premium" is the payment made to the insurance company. The total or annual premium is often broken down into an annual, semi-annual, or monthly payment schedule. The most common is semi-annual and monthly. Fees vary for each different payment schedule. Check with your insurance company to see which payment schedule either eliminates the fee or lowers it.

"Deductible" is the amount you pay out of pocket to cover the costs of an accident before the insurance company pays anything. Common dollar levels for deductibles are $100, $250, $500, and $1,000—the higher your deductible the lower your premiums. To determine which deductible is right for you there are two questions you need to ask. First, can I cover the cost of the deductible I select? There is no point choosing a high deductible if you can't cover it if an accident occurs. Second, how much do my premiums vary with each deductible? Choosing a high deductible can greatly reduce your premiums allowing you to save hundreds of dollars each year. Once you know the answer to both questions, you can choose a deductible that is correct for you.

"Bodily injury liability" covers damage or injuries to third parties that are your fault. If you injure or kill someone in an automobile accident, and it's your fault, you will be sued for damages. Third parties can take away certain types of property from you if you can't pay their damage claims. Make sure you carry enough liability insurance to protect yourself and your property from legal judgments.

"Comprehensive" covers your vehicle for losses resulting from incidents other than collision. For example, it covers damage to your car if it is stolen; or damaged by flood, fire, or animals. To keep your premiums low, select as high a deductible as you feel comfortable paying out of pocket.

"Collision" covers damage to your car resulting from an accident. Lower your premium on this type of coverage by choosing the highest deductible you can afford. For older cars, consider dropping this coverage, since coverage is normally limited to the cash value of your car. While states don't require this type of coverage, whomever you took your car loan with will want you to have this type of insurance.

Other types of car insurances include medical, property and various types of under-insurances. Check these out with your auto insurance company.

We want you to read your car insurance policy. While we can't promise you that it makes for exciting reading, it will tell you your existing auto insurance coverage. One confusing notation used in auto insurance contracts appears as two numbers separated by a slash. For example, you might see 50/100 or 100/300. Assuming the 100/300 refers is to bodily injury coverage it means $100,000 per injury with a maximum payout of $300,000.

Compare auto insurance costs with several insurance companies to make sure you're getting the best coverage for the least cost. Be careful when comparing policies. Make sure you are comparing apples to apples and not apples to oranges. It's easy to think that you're getting a great deal on an auto insurance policy when in fact you're not being properly protected.

Life Insurance

Life insurance replaces lost income after a wage earner dies and covers bills and other expenses left by the deceased. Many insurance agents recommend you carry life insurance equal to eight to ten times your annual income. We're less mechanical in our recommendation. We want you to calculate your debt obligations (mortgage, credit cards, student loans, etc.) combined with the dollar amount needed to replace your income. After you do this you might discover you need less or more coverage than the eight to ten times income recommendation.

Here is an example of a family situation and their insurance need.

Sam is married to Julie and they have two young children. Sam earns $50,000 per year. Julie is a full-time mom. Sam's employer has a group life policy that is worth two times his annual salary or $100,000.

Sam and Julie's debt includes:

1.	Outstanding Mortgage	$125,000
2.	Two cars loans	40,000
3.	Combined student loans	45,000
	Total debt	$210,000

In order to calculate the investment amount needed to replace Sam's income, we need to multiply his annual salary by 17. This multiplier is a simple way to estimate what Julie will need to replace Sam's salary assuming a 6% (1 ÷ .06 ≈ 17) annual return on invested insurance money. If you assumed a 5% annual return then the multiplier would be 20 (1 ÷ .05 = 20).

17 x $50,000 = $850,000

Now we need to add Sam and Julie's debt to this $850,000, which comes to $1,060,000.

Given Sam's employer provides him with $100,000 of life insurance he will need to add a little over $900,000 of additional life insurance.

One thing we ignored in this illustration is how Sam's family needs will change overtime. For example, Sam's $50,000 salary might be okay now but might prove too little as his children age and go to college. How your family's income requirement changes with time is something you need to consider.

Life insurance isn't for everyone, though. If you have zero dependents and no liabilities, then why carry life insurance? However, if you have debt that someone needed to co-sign for you might want life insurance so that your co-signer isn't left responsible for your debt.

Types of Life Insurance

The two primary types of life insurance are term and whole life. Life insurance products are structured in a variety of ways. Most whole life products will take a portion of your monthly premium and invest that money and over time, the policy owner will build up a cash value. Term policies do not have a cash value, but the cost is about one twelfth of whole life. If you had a whole life policy that has a premium of $250 per month ($3,000/year), a term policy with the exact same coverage would cost $250 for entire year.

For most people, the best form of life insurance is term. In term insurance, you pay premiums to your insurance company and upon death; your beneficiaries receive a check. Term insurance has no savings or investments built into it. This makes term insurance the cheapest form of life insurance you can buy.

"Term" insurance can be purchased in two different ways, annual renewable or level premium. Here is how each works. Annual renewable policies will increase your premium each year by a small amount. The older you get the more the premium. Level premium will set your annual payment at the same amount for a specific number of years. The set periods could be five, ten, or twenty years. What that means is that you would have the same annual payment for the entire number of years that you selected. This method will increase your annual cost, but it will leave you with knowing how much you will have to pay each year for an extended period of time.

"Whole Life" insurance combines a guaranteed death benefit with a guaranteed cash value that builds overtime. Premiums on a whole life policy are higher than term insurance and its premium never increases. One issue with whole life is that the effective return you receive on its cash value is low relative to other investment options. We think you're better off sticking to term and investing in other types of financial assets than whole life. Most whole life policies will include a minimum guarantee on the cash account in the range of about 3 to 4 percent.

One twist on whole life insurance is variable whole life that invests your account in financial assets whose value fluctuates. Your policy's cash value isn't guaranteed—your account will outperform a traditional whole life policy if the stock market is going up and will underperform it if the market heads south. Universal is another form of variable life insurance policies that will invest that cash value into the market. Those investment choices will depend on the insurance company. Index universal life insurance works the same as variable but they will invest in a specific index, which makes the management fee on this type of policy a little lower than actively managed funds.

Most financial planners recommend term life insurance to their clients because you can get the same life insurance coverage as a whole life policy at a lower cost and invest the difference in a way that earns higher returns than a whole life policy.

Comparison of "Whole" and "Term" Life Insurance

> Joe is 30 years old and he needs $500,000 worth of life insurance.
>
> If Joe goes with a whole life policy is annual premium is $3,000. After ten years, the cash value of his policy is worth $10,000. Remember, he has paid in $30,000.
>
> Joe could have purchased the same amount of death benefit through term insurance for an annual premium is $250. This would allow Joe to invest $2,750 each year (the $3,000 - $250). Assuming a 7% return, Joe's investment would be worth $40,000 at the end of 10 years.
>
> What would you rather have after ten years: $10,000 or $40,000?
>
> The problem with whole life insurance is that the insurance company keeps the majority of your premium and only invests a small part of it.

Calculating your Life Insurance Needs

Go through our life insurance checklist below. Check all boxes that apply.

Yes	No	
❑	❑	Are you married?
❑	❑	Do you have children?
❑	❑	Do you have debt?
❑	❑	Do you need to save for the cost of your funeral?
		(Average funeral costs are thousands of dollars)
❑	❑	Can you afford to purchase a cemetery plot?

If you answer yes to one or more question then you probably need life insurance. Each of you should have enough life insurance to pay all your debt and funeral expenses, and have enough left over to invest to replace lost income.

If you're single and you don't have children, then life insurance probably isn't for you. If you have debt and your parents must pay for your funeral and cemetery plot, then life insurance might make sense.

For most of people, the best type of life insurance to own is term.

How much life insurance should you have? Many experts suggest coverage equal to eight to ten times your annual income. As mentioned earlier, the amount you'll need depends on your family's financial situation.

Below is a rough guide to help you plan your life insurance needs. We ignore tax related issues.

Life Insurance Needs

Debts		Assets	
Outstanding Mortgage	_____	401K	_____
Car Loans	_____	IRA's	_____
Credit card balances	_____	Savings	_____
Other debt	_____	Other	_____
Total Debt	_____	Total Assets	_____

Current life insurance coverage _____ + Assets _____ =
Current coverage_____

Annual income you want to replace _____ × 20 (assumes 5% return on invested insurance money) = _____ + Total debt_____ + Funeral costs _____ = Life insurance needed

_____

Total amount of insurance needed minus current amount of coverage equals the insurance coverage your short. This is how much additional life insurance you need to buy.

Life insurance needed _____ − Current coverage
_____ = Amount of insurance you need to add

_____

If you're current coverage is greater than what you need consider reducing your coverage and invest the money you save.

Disability Insurance

Disability insurance covers your wage if you injure yourself and can't work or not earn as much as you were before the injury. Every working adult should have disability insurance. Almost every worker has some form of disability coverage—either through workers' compensation, Social Security, veterans' insurance, or employer paid coverage. You should have enough disability insurance to cover your family's expenses if you can't work or earn as much as you previously earned.

Disability insurance is additional coverage over and above what your employer pays into workers compensation or Social Security. There are two types of disability insurance—short-term and long-term. Short-term disability covers you for the first six months of being disabled. Long-term disability typically begins after the first six months.

If you have an accident that's not work related you couldn't collect workers compensation. To qualify for disability under Social Security you'll have to prove that you're permanently unable to work. Disability insurance fills the void that workers compensation and Social Security doesn't cover. For example, you fall off the roof of your home leaving you injured and unable to work. Disability insurance will pay you around 60 percent of your income while you're disabled.

We're strong promoters of having disability insurance. Statistically you're more likely to need disability insurance more than life insurance yet most people never think about their disability coverage.

If you are self-employed, you can purchase a disability insurance to support your business losses while you are unable to work. These types of policies would be designed to replace most or all of your business income if you were not able to work. While personal disability policies are designed for longer periods of time—five years or up to you reaching age sixty-five, business disability policies will cover a shorter time, only a couple of years. You can extend the time, but it will also cost you in a higher premium.

If you do work for a company, most will offer a disability policy for an inexpensive price, ten to twenty dollars per month. If you are purchasing a policy on your own the cost would be two to three hundred per month, depending on your income.

Calculating your Disability Insurance Needs

What would happen to your family if you became disabled and couldn't work? Becoming disabled is more likely than dying; yet often we ignore our disability insurance needs. How much disability insurance do you need? Again, this depends on the particulars of your life. Does your spouse work? Can his or her paycheck sustain your household? The purpose of disability insurance is to help maintain a decent standard of living if you can't work.

First, calculate your current disability insurance coverage:

Short-term Disability Insurance: $ _____
Long-term Disability Insurance: $ _____
Workers' Compensation: $_____

(This varies from state to state and is purchased by your employer. Self-employed individuals must buy it for themselves.)

Social Security: $ _____
(Yes, social security offers some coverage for permanent disability.)
Veterans' Disability Insurance: $ _____
Total $ _____

Be careful in interpreting your total. Some of these sources of disability insurance are not paid if other sources of disability insurance are present. If this coverage is still inadequate, you can often buy disability insurance from your trade or professional associations or private insurers.

Health Insurance

(We're ignoring coverage offered by President Obama's healthcare initiative. Too many issues surrounding this program are still unsettled. To learn about the president's initiative go to www.whitehouse.gov/healthreform.)

Health insurance pays your medical expenses. If you don't have health insurance, it's difficult to care for your health needs. For many Americans, their employer provides health insurance at a reasonable cost. If you have to buy health insurance on your own, it's more costly. Even with health insurance, you're going to have medical expenses. Health insurance policies almost never cover the full cost of medical treatment.

How much medical insurance do you need? This depends on a host of variables unique to you and its affordability. Everyone needs medical insurance. Here's a list of benefits that accrue to having health insurance:

1. With health insurance, you're more likely to be able to afford expensive medical care.
2. Health insurance can pay for services that you use often such as prescription medicines.

3. Health insurance can help you to get better quality care as a member of a coordinated health plan.
4. With health insurance, you worry less about the cost of care when you're sick.
5. The additional money provided by health insurance when you're sick is more valuable to you than those same dollars when you're well.
6. You don't pay income tax on health insurance benefits so it is more valuable per dollar than the same amount in taxable pay.
7. Health insurance companies generally pay lower prices to doctors and hospitals than you would pay on your own.

Medical Savings Account (MSA)

An MSA is a type of account some employers offer. An MSA is a savings account (no interest is paid) funded from your paycheck on a pre-tax basis used for medical expenses you incur such as medicine, co-pays, dental, medical, or even vitamins. If you're in the 15 percent tax bracket this means that every $85 dollars you save in an MSA provides you with $100 of medical cost purchasing power. Money not used in the account by the end of the year is lost. The purpose of an MSA is to complement your health insurance and not replace it.

Recording Names and Addresses of your Insurance Agents and Companies

As ridiculous as it sounds, in times of emergencies people often can't find the name and telephone number of their insurance agents and insurance companies. Before an emergency strikes, record this information and put it in a safe and accessible place.

(In fact, we suggest you create a comprehensive list of all bank accounts, investment accounts (retirement and non-retirement), your lawyer and accountant's names and numbers, and any other important information.)

Follow the below format for insurance agents and companies:

Insurance type: _____ (you fill in)

	Name	_____
	Phone	_____
	Address	_____
		_____

Insurance type: _____ (you fill in)

	Name	_____
	Phone	_____
	Address	_____
		_____

Insurance type: _____ (you fill in)

              Name   _____

              Phone   _____

              Address   _____

                            _____

Insurance type: _____ (you fill in)

              Name   _____

              Phone   _____

              Address   _____

                              _____

HOME OWNERSHIP

If there is a rock upon which American investment advice is built, it is that the first asset you should acquire is your own home. The largest financial benefit from home ownership is that instead of paying rent, you are paying off a mortgage that will result in the acquisition of an asset. Other financial benefits involve special tax deductions for homeowners, protection against rent increases, the ability to borrow against your home's equity, et cetera. Home ownership's downsides include the need to raise down payment money (that could be invested in other places), mortgage interest payments, property taxes, the need for more home insurance, and upkeep expenses.

Two critical variables in deciding whether to buy or rent is how long you plan to live in the home and the rent you're paying. The shorter the duration of your residence and the lower your rent, the more renting makes sense.

Mortgages

There are several types of mortgages lenders offer and it is important for you to understand their differences. The type of mortgage we recommend for most borrowers is a fixed rate, fifteen- or thirty-year mortgage. The interest rate on a fixed rate mortgage never changes.

A variable rate mortgage has an interest rate that varies based on some key market rate. If this key rate goes up so will your mortgage payment. If it goes down so will your mortgage payment. We believe that variable rate mortgages are too risky for the average homeowner.

One question you need to answer when shopping for a mortgage is whether you want a fifteen- or thirty-year mortgage. Fifteen-year mortgages normally carry a lower interest rate and reduce the total cost of your home loan. Of course, a fifteen-year mortgage also means greater monthly payments. Keep in mind that most thirty-year mortgages can be paid-off quicker without penalty by simply paying more each month.

You should be very cautious of real estate agents who try to sell you a more expensive house than what you can afford and try to make your mortgage payment affordable by sticking you with a thirty-year mortgage. Don't play this game. It is important to understand that real estate agents don't necessarily have your best interests in mind when selling you a house.

We recommend that before you go shopping for a house you predetermine what you are willing to spend and communicate this clearly to your real estate agent. We advise couples to buy a house that one of their incomes can afford. Given today's economic uncertainties, buying a house that requires two salaries to pay-off is a mistake.

Below is an example that illustrates the cost differences between a fifteen- and thirty-year mortgage. We use a 6 percent and 6.5 percent rate in our illustration. Currently, mortgage rates are much less. The rates used do not affect the point of our illustration.

---

15 Versus 30-Year Mortgage

Assume a 15-year, $150,000 mortgage with an interest rate of 6%. Its principal and interest payment will be $1265.79.

Total payments:	$1,265.79 x 180 (15 yrs x 12) = $227,842.20
Total interest on loan:	$ 227,842.20 – 150,000 = $77,872.20

Assume a 30-year, $150,000 mortgage with an interest rate of 6.5% (notice the higher interest charge). Its principal and interest payment is $948.10.

Total payments:	$948.10 x 360 (30 yrs x 12) = 341,316.00.
The total interest on loan:	$341,316.00 – 150,000 = $191,316

THE 15-YEAR MORTAGE COMPARED TO THE 30-YEAR SAVES THE BORROWER APPROXIMATELY $113,437 ($191,316 – $77,872).

What could you do with this extra $113,437? One thing is to help build a secure retirement.

Live within your means and buy a home that you can afford to stay with a 15-year mortgage.

CALCULATE YOUR PROJECTED SOCIAL SECURITY INCOME

Most people don't read their annual Social Security Administration state-ment. Mailed to you yearly this statement tells you how much you earned for the year and your projected retirement benefits. You need this infor-mation to do your financial planning.

You can order a statement online at www.socialsecurity.gov.

CREDIT CARDS

A credit card is a short-term cash substitute and not a long-term, high-interest rate, loan. Credit card purchases can help build your credit rating if you use them wisely. This means that every month you pay your card purchases in full. As a loan, credit card money is a bad deal because it car-ries a very high interest rate. If you can't afford to pay cash for what you are about to purchase on a credit card then you shouldn't be buying it!

Seven Steps to Pay-off Credit Card Debt

1. Develop a payoff plan by determining the maximum amount of money you can afford to pay each month. If you make minimum payments on your credit card debt then it will take forever to pay it off, and you'll be paying exorbitant amounts of money in interest and fees—money that could be put toward paying down your credit card balance.
2. Go online and find a credit card payment calculator. We previously recommended a site.
3. If you owe money on more than one credit card then first pay-down the card with the smallest balance, or consider debt consolidation. Debt consolidation is when you borrow money to payoff all your credit cards at once. You then have to pay back the money you borrowed. Sometimes these debt consolidation loans carry a lower interest rate than credit card debt and most people find it easier to make a single payment than making multiple payments on multiple cards.
4. Build your monthly credit card expenses into your budget.
5. Don't add to your credit card debt if you have outstanding balances that you can't payoff.
6. Never ignore a credit card payment. If you can't make a payment then call your credit card company and explain why. Try to arrange a payment plan that fits your budget.

7. Don't be afraid to call your credit card company and ask for a lower interest rate. Credit card companies want your business. Sometimes, especially if you haven't missed a payment, you can negotiate a lower interest rate.

Six Credit Card Tips

1. It's okay to use a credit card as a cash substitute or for emergencies. Never use your credit card as a long-term loan.
2. Search online for the best credit card rates.
3. Each month payoff your credit card balances in full. Don't charge anything to a credit card that you can't afford to pay for with cash.
4. Avoid all phony promotional or introductory credit card offers.
5. Always read a credit card's contract. We know it's small print and often written in gobbledygook. If you think you're mature enough to use a credit card then you're mature enough to read its contract.
6. Avoid the minimum payment trap. Make payments on your credit card that are sufficient to pay it off in a reasonable amount of time.

Treating Card Debt Seriously

The average American is many thousands of dollars in credit card debt—don't join them. Credit card debt will eat you alive and prevent you from ever building wealth. That's why we want you to pay-off all of your credit card debt before you start a savings and investment program.

FICO Score

Linked closely to credit card debt is your FICO score. FICO stands for Fair Isaac Corporation, its developer, and is a credit score that measures your credit worthiness. It tells lenders your ability to pay back loans.

The Lowdown on FICO
- FICO scores range from 300 to 850. We recommend that you strive for a 750 FICO score or at worst, something in the low 700 hundreds.
- The higher your score the better your credit risk.
- You're entitled to one free credit report within a twelve-month period from each of the credit bureaus: Equifax, Experian, and TransUnion.
- A credit report describes your credit history and determines your FICO score. It describes each of your credit lines and their status (i.e., how much you owe). It also reports public financial records such as bankruptcies, judgments, and tax liens against—all of which hurt your FICO score.

How to Increase Your FICO Score
- Pay your bills when due.
- Use only a small percentage of your available credit. Avoid using more than 25 percent of any credit line. For example, if you credit card limit is $4,000 then don't carry balances greater than $1,000.
- Try to avoid shortening the length of your credit card history by taking on new debt that lowers the average age of your accounts. As an illustration: you currently have one credit card that is four years old. Thus the average age of this account is four years. Now you acquire a new credit card. The average age of both cards is now two years [(4 + 0) ÷ 2 = 2]. This can lower your FICO score.
- Don't become a collector of credit cards. Too many cards cause lenders to worry that you might spend yourself into oblivion. If you want to collect cards, stick to baseball.
- Minimize your revolving and installment loans. A revolving loan (e.g., credit card) has a credit limit and when you payoff the loan your credit limit returns to its previous level. An installment loan (e.g., car loan) is for a fixed amount and you are given a payment schedule that will eventually bring your loan amount back to zero. Revolving loans carry a higher interest charge than an installment loan.
- Don't close out a credit card even if you plan on never using it again. When you close a credit line, you increase your credit utilization rate that then hurts your FICO score.

7

✝

Basic Types of Paper Financial Assets

STOCKS

Beginning with this chapter and ending with chapter 11, we work at building your financial vocabulary. Be patient while reading this material—there's a lot to learn. The best way to see this vocabulary in action is to watch the nightly business and investing TV shows. This will reinforce and demonstrate the importance of the terms you're studying.

Stocks or equity shares represent ownership in a company. Investors buy stock to earn dividends and capital appreciation. Dividends are profits earned by a company and distributed to stockholders on a per share basis. If you own one hundred shares of IBM stock and a twenty-five cent dividend is paid you'll receive $25 (0.25 x 100). Capital gain is when the market value of a share of stock rises. If you buy a share of stock for $10 and later sell it for $15, you earn a $5 capital gain. Total return adds together capital gains and dividends. Average annual

return is how much you make from an investment each year expressed
as a percentage.

To learn how to make these calculations, study the example below.

How to Calculate Capital Gain or Appreciation, Total Return and Average Annual Return
on a Single Share of Stock

Bob purchases a single share of stock for $25 and sells it four years later for $40. This
stock also pays a quarterly dividend of 25¢ per share.

What is Bob's capital gain? Price Sold – Price Paid = Capital Gain (if this is a negative
number it would be a capital loss) = $40 – $25 = $15

Capital Gain = $15 or expressed as a percentage $15/$25 = 60%

What is Bob's total return? He receives a 25¢ dividend four times a year for four years
for a total dividend payout of $4. Add this to Bob's capital gain for a total return of $19.
To express this as a percentage divide the $19 by his initial investment of $25.

Total Return %= (Dividends + Capital Gain) ÷ Price Paid = $19/$25 = 76%

What is Bob's average annual return? Total return as a percentage divided by 4 (years) or
19%.

Average Annual Return = 76%/4 = 19%

Two categories of stock exist: common and preferred. Both represent
ownership in a company. Preferred stock has priority over common stock
in the payment of dividends and upon liquidation of a corporation's assets. However, common stocks participate more widely in a company's
profit and, thus, show more capital appreciation than preferred. In addition, preferred stock holders usually don't have voting rights. Preferred
stock has characteristics of both debt (e.g., fixed dividends) and equity
(potential appreciation). Whenever we refer to *stock*, we'll mean *common*.

A large vocabulary exists to describe the characteristics of common
stock. As you study investing, you'll see references to:

- Income stock: purchased for dividend income. Income stock is associated with established, slower growing companies and utilities such
  as electric companies.
- Penny stock: priced below $5 per share and sells in the over-the-
  counter market. Penny stock isn't considered an investment grade
  asset.
- Blue chip stock: issued by well-established companies. Blue chip
  stocks trade in major financial markets such as the New York Stock
  Exchange.
- Growth stock: purchased for capital appreciation. Growth stock is
  linked to faster growing companies.

- Value stock: stock undervalued by the market. Investors purchase value stock to achieve capital appreciation. Some spectacularly successful investors, like Warren Buffet, are value investors.
- Cyclical stock: stock's price moves with the US business cycle. The business cycle is when the economy's output is expanding or receding. The price of cyclical stock moves either with or against these expansions and recessions. During expansions, the price of pro-cyclical stock rises while the price of counter-cyclical stock declines.
- Small-cap and large-cap stocks: refers to the total dollar market value of a company's outstanding stock shares. Small-cap companies have a smaller total market value than large-cap. Often linked to rapid capital appreciation.

BONDS

Bonds are debt instruments. When you lend money to either a private company (e.g., Motorola) or to a public entity (e.g., Detroit), they issue you a bond. When you purchase a bond, you become a lender. As a lender, the borrower promises to pay you back your principal and interest.

Principal is the money you lent and interest is the money promised in return for lending. Bondholders do not share in the profit of a company and in the case of bankruptcy have a prior claim on assets before stock investors.

Types of Bonds

Three types of bonds exist: corporate, municipal, and Treasury. Private companies issue corporate bonds to pay for plant modernization and to cover operating expenses. States, cities, towns, and counties sell municipal bonds. Municipal bonds finance bridges, schools, highways, and other public works. The US Department of the Treasury sells Treasury bonds to finance the federal government's deficit. In the United States, when the federal government spends more that it receives from taxes, it must borrow money to make up this deficit. Treasury bonds serve this task. The accumulation of past deficits equals our national debt.

CASH

Cash refers to cash equivalents assets. Cash equivalent assets are liquid debt instruments. Liquidity refers to how easy an investor can change an asset into money. Examples of cash equivalent assets are CDs (i.e., certificates of deposit), T-bills (i.e., Treasury bills), checking and savings accounts, and commercial paper (used by companies to finance short-term cash flow needs).

OTHER TYPES OF FINANCIAL ASSETS

Many other types of financial assets exist. Three types frequently mentioned in the media are futures, options, and real estate investment trusts (REITS). For the average investor, futures and options carry too much risk to consider as an investment.

A futures contract is a promise to buy or sell something in the future. Traditionally, futures contracts traded commodities such as corn or soybean. Today future contracts include financial futures on currencies, securities, and intangible assets such as stock indexes.

One practical way that business uses future contracts is to lock in future prices. A candy company (e.g., Hershey) might want to guarantee itself the price of sugar six months in the future. A way of accomplishing this is to buy a futures contract on sugar at a specified price.

An option is a contract between a buyer and a seller that gives the buyer of the option the right to buy or to sell something before a date at an agreed price, called the strike price. In return for selling the option, the seller collects a payment called a premium.

Options come in two basic flavors: call and put. A call option gives the buyer the right to buy something and a put option gives the buyer the right to sell something. If the buyer of the option chooses to exercise this right, the seller is obliged to either sell or buy what the buyer wants at the strike price.

Stock options give the buyer the right to buy or sell shares of common stock. Each options contract controls one hundred shares of stock. The strike price of an option is its selling price. When you purchase a call stock option (the right to buy something), you're betting that the price of the stock will rise above its strike price. The higher the price goes above its strike price the more valuable the option because you can now buy stock at its cheaper price (i.e., strike price) and sell it at its higher market price. If the stock's price falls below its strike price, the option becomes worthless.

When you buy a put option (this is the right to sell something), you're betting the price of the stock will drop below its strike price. When this happens, you can buy the stock at below its strike price and then sell it at its strike price.

Real Estate Investment Trusts or REITs pool investment money and purchase and manage real estate properties like hotels, malls, commercial, and industrial properties. REITs trade on major exchanges like stock and pay yields in the form of dividends and can change in value. REITs offer investors a low cost and liquid way of investing in real property.

REITs are often a good investment for people looking for income. One thing to be careful of when investing in REITs is that their value can be sensitive to interest rates. When interest rates go up the value of a REIT normally goes down and vice-versa.

NON-PAPER ASSETS

A list of common real (i.e., tangible) assets that may either complement or substitute for financial (i.e., paper) assets are home ownership, precious metals, collectibles, diamonds, real estate, and business ownership.

From this list, we only recommend home ownership. Real estate—this is different from home ownership—can be a good investment as part of a well-diversified portfolio, but the average person should hold it as a REIT. Only experts should invest in diamonds, precious metals, and collectibles. Over the last twenty years, owning your own business has become popular. A business isn't a savings asset.

8

✛

The Basic
Language of Investing

It's important to understand the difference between investing and gambling. Investing always links an investment decision with a final goal. A final goal is rational if it's reachable with a moderate level of risk. Gambling is entertainment and too risky of a strategy to secure your future. Regrettably, many financial firms try to sell investors high-risk assets with the allure of a quick fortune. Avoid them. "Get rich quick schemes" involve too much risk and, therefore, fall into the category of gambling.

Investors have to understand return, risk, and diversification. Return measures earnings from investing. Risk calculates the "chance" dimension of investing—you can make or lose money. This is one of the costs of investing. Diversification is a strategy to reduce risk by investing in a variety of different asset classes in different industries and countries.

RETURN

Return refers to what you earn on an investment. As stated earlier, stocks earn dividends and capital gain. The dividend received per share of stock is its dividend payout. Dividend payout divided by the stock's market price—what you have to pay to buy it—equals its dividend yield. If you add a stock's capital appreciation, stated as a percentage, you have a stock's total return.

(Dividend Payout) ÷ (Stock's Market Value) = Dividend Yield
(Dividend Yield) + (Capital Appreciation as a percentage) = Total Return as Percentage

Assume you own a share of Microsoft stock. This year, its dividend payout is fifty cents per share. If the market value of a share of Microsoft is $10, then its dividend yield equals:

($0.50) ÷ ($10) = 5%

Assuming the price of the stock appreciated 10 percent, total return on this investment would be 15 percent (5 percent dividend yield + 10 percent appreciation).

When examining returns on bonds, a more complicated picture arises. Here you have to calculate a coupon yield, current yield, and yield to maturity. Many types of bonds have a coupon payment. A coupon payment is money the bond issuer promises to pay, usually semi-annually, to the bondholder. Dividing a bond's coupon payment by its par value—which is its face value or stated value—determines its coupon yield.

(Coupon Payment) ÷ (Bond's Par Value) = Coupon Yield

Dividing a bond's coupon payment by its market value gives you its current yield.

(Coupon Payment) ÷ (Bond's Market Value) = Current Yield

Suppose you buy a corporate bond and the bond's par value, which is the bond's stated or face value, is $1,000. The bond has a coupon yield of 10%, which means each year you'll receive $100. This is the bond's coupon payment. Here the bond's coupon yield equals:

($100) ÷ ($1,000) = 10%

Bonds can sell at face value (e.g., $1,000), below face value or above face value. Face value is what a bondholder will receive from a borrower when the bond fully matures on its due date. If a bond sells below face value, it sells at a discount. If you buy a bond at discount, then its current yield will be greater than its coupon yield. When a bond sells for above face value, it's selling at a premium. Bonds purchased at a premium will have a current yield below its coupon yield. If a bond is purchased at face value then its coupon and current yields will be the same.

As an example, let's say you buy a bond that has a face value of $1,000 for $900. In this case, the bond sold at a $100 discount. To calculate the bond's current yield, divide its coupon payment (assume $100 from previous example) by its (current) market price:

($100) ÷ ($900) = 11%

In this example, the bond's current yield is greater than its coupon yield of 10 percent.

The yield to maturity calculates a bond's yield, taking into account any capital gain or loss and assuming all coupon payments are reinvested at the bond's current yield. For a bond held to maturity, yield to maturity matters most. The math necessary to calculate yield to maturity is beyond the scope of our materials. Online calculators exist that make this calculation for you: www.financeformulas.net/Yield_to_Maturity.html#Calc-Header.

However, here is a quick and dirty formula for calculating yield to maturity:

$$\text{Yield to Maturity} = \frac{C + (F - P) \div N}{(F + P) \div 2}$$

C = Coupon payment
F = Face value of bond
P = Price of bond
N = Years to maturity

Let's look at an example. You buy a $1,000 bond for $900. Its coupon payment is $50 per year. The bond matures in ten years.

Coupon yield equals:

$50 ÷ $1000 = 5%.

Current yield equals

$50 ÷ $900 ≈ 5.6% (rounded).

Yield to maturity equals

$$\frac{\$50 + (\$1000 - \$900) \div 10}{(\$1,000 + \$900) \div 2} \approx 6.3\%.$$

Historical Returns on Assets

Through the twentieth century and during the first ten years of the twenty-first century, stocks, on average, over this entire span of time, have outperformed bonds and bonds have outperformed cash assets. The numbers clearly show this: stocks 9.3 percent, corporate bonds 5.65 percent, and Treasury T-bills 3.91 percent. Just to complete this picture, property has returned 3.42 percent and gold 3.7 percent. These are all nominal returns—this means they have not been adjusted for inflation.

More recently, from 2003 to 2012, stocks have returned 8.84 percent, corporate bonds 6.49 percent, and Treasury bills 3.14 percent.

If you invested $1 in the stock market in 1800, by 2010, assuming 9.3 percent return, you would have $140,881,566. The same dollar invested in corporate bonds would now be worth $108,759. And if you invested your money with the government (e.g., Treasury bills) then you would have $3,271.

We know what you're thinking, long-term, why would anyone invest in anything but stocks. Don't interpret this data as evidence against ever investing in anything but stock. Debt instruments and cash assets still have a place in your portfolio depending on your savings goals and current economic conditions. It does strongly suggest, however, that a long-term investor weigh their portfolio toward stock.

RISK

Financial returns are random variables. Random variables take on a range of different values. Financial risk measures the spread on possible financial returns. Below are yearly possible returns on a share of Izzy Dizzy stock.

Possible Returns on a Share of Izzy Dizzy Stock:

<-->
        –5% –2% 0% +3% +7% +10%

Risk is the spread on these possibilities. One measure of risk is to subtract a spread's lowest value from its highest value.

(Highest Return) – (Lowest Return) = Risk

In this example, risk equals:

(10%) – (-5%) = 15%

This means that during any given year you could earn as much as 10 percent and lose as much as 5 percent—a possible swing of 15 percent.

Below is the same type of information for a share of Nadlerbabble stock.

Returns on a Share of Nadlerbabble Stock:

<-->
        –2% 0 +7%

Here, risk equals:

(7%) – (–2%) = 9%

Nadler babble's lower risk number indicates less spread in potential returns, which gives investors more confidence in earning their expected return.

Historical Measures of Risk

During the twentieth century, common stocks' highest one-year annual real return was 56.8 percent and its lowest –38 percent. This gives us a risk measure of 94.8 percent (56.8% – (–38%)). Bonds highest one-year annual real return was 35.1 percent and its lowest was –19.3 percent for a risk measure of 54.1 percent. For Treasury bills, its highest one-year return was 20 percent and its lowest –15.1 percent for a risk measure of 35.1 percent.

Using a more sophisticated measure of risk called standard deviation, during this same time period, stocks had a standard deviation of 20.2 percent, bonds 10.2 percent, and Treasury bills 4.7 percent.

Combining this information with historical returns gives us a more complete picture of the trade-offs between investing in stocks, bonds, and cash assets. In financial investing, you pay for higher returns by exposing yourself to additional risk. The cost of avoiding risk is lower return.

As an investor, you have to choose some combination of risk and return that lets you sleep at night and accomplish your financial goals.

DIVERSIFICATION

The most important insight in investing is the need to distribute your savings among different classes of financial assets. This is diversification. As an illustration, take the case of a thirty-year-old who is thirty-five years away from retiring. A possible portfolio for this individual might contain 50 percent American common stocks, 30 percent international stocks and 20 percent bonds. This spreading-out of savings reduces portfolio risk because in some years American common stocks do well while international common stocks do poorly and in some years bonds outperform stocks. In any one typical year, this portfolio will contain winners and losers. Over time, this causes financial returns to behave in a steadier (i.e., less risky) manner. Diversification can reduce your risk, but never eliminate it.

The time series below illustrates the diversification insight.

Return in investments A and B are plotted against time beginning with 1948. Returns on A and B fluctuate around 10 percent. This movement represents risk. Their individual long-term average return is 10 percent.

Assume we combine A and B into a single portfolio. Now compare their individual movements with their combined movements (A and B) as

Chapter 8

Diversification Insight

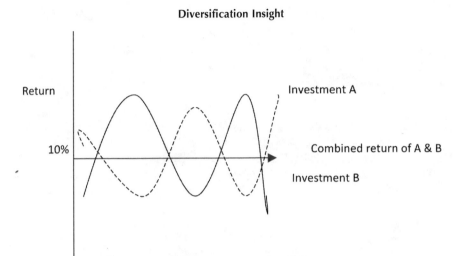

Figure 8.1. Diversification of two investments and return.

represented by the solid horizontal line with the arrowhead. Combined, they have a steady return of 10 percent. This is counter-intuitive: combine two risky assets and you reduce risk. Its explanation, though, is simple: when you combine two risky assets whose returns move in opposite direction, you cancel their individual risk.

9

+

Factors that Affect Return

RISK

How does risk affect return? Most investors are risk averse. This means that investors require compensation for their risk exposure. Financial assets with greater risk pay higher returns.

The graph below reflects the trade-offs between risk and return.

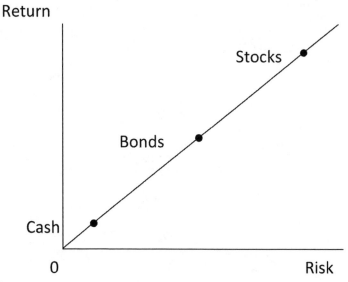

Figure 9.1.   Risk and Return Trade-off.

The vertical axis measures return and the horizontal axis risk. Low risk assets, like cash equivalents, have low returns; high-risk assets, such as stock, pay high returns. This is the nature of investing: if you want to earn higher returns, you must expose yourself to more risk.

Review our discussion of historical measures of risk (in chapter 8). Stocks have the highest return and greatest risk, followed by bonds, and then cash equivalents. Figure 8.1 shows this relationship.

INFLATION

Inflation has a complicated relationship with financial returns. Inflation occurs when the prices of goods and services rise. Take the case of a Hershey bar—something dear to our hearts. In 1962, a Hershey bar cost $0.05. By 1994, that same bar cost $0.75. This represents a price increase of 1,400 percent. Over the same time, McDonald's double burger increased in price from $0.28 to $1.65; a full-size Chevrolet from $2,529 to $19,495; and a gallon of gasoline from $0.31 to $1.19 per gallon.

Inflation reduces the purchasing power of money. A dollar in 1962 could buy twenty Hershey bars or almost four McDonald's double burgers. That same dollar today buys just one Hershey bar and not a single McDonald's double burger.

How does this relate to your financial goals? Let's say you decide to begin saving for your four-year-old daughter's college education. You would like her to attend your alma mater that today costs around $20,000 a year. If no inflation exists, you can be reasonably sure that its future cost will be similar to what it is today. (Actually, the cost of higher education is rising more rapidly than the inflation rate. The price of a public university education has risen by 42 percent over the past ten years.) Now, assume an inflation rate of 3 percent per year. How will this affect the cost of your daughter's college education? It will increase it by at least $10,000. This means that you must save more to achieve this goal.

This process is even worse when saving over decades. Say grandparents want to begin a savings plan for a grandchild with a target amount of wealth equal to $1,000,000 in fifty years. Assume a 10 percent return with no inflation. They would have to begin saving about $860 a year. Now let's recalculate assuming an inflation rate of 3 percent per year. The amount jumps to around $2,460 a year.

The extent to which inflation affects your financial returns depends on the types of assets you hold and the length of time you're invested. During short time periods, stocks and bonds are unable to adjust their returns to offset inflation. Cash assets, being shorter term and more liquid, adjust their returns more rapidly. During the 1970s, when the US economy suffered a high rate of inflation, investments in stocks and bonds were unable to protect their real purchasing power. (During this period, tangible assets such as land, gold, art, etc. did quite well.)

Over longer time-periods, however, stock investments are able to offset the effects of inflation through adjustments to their returns, while bonds and cash assets don't.

TAXES AND COMMISSIONS

Taxes, like death, are unavoidable. Taxes on financial income and capital gain reduce real financial returns. The golden rule of investing is to avoid taxes whenever possible. In a later chapter, we discuss how to do this through tax shelters.

Taxes on investment capital gains differ based on the length of time you hold an investment. The Internal Revenue Service defines a long-term investment as something owned for more than one year and a short-term investment as one held for less than one year. The current tax rates for long-term capital gains are either 15 percent or 20 percent depending on your tax bracket, while short-term capital gains are taxed at the same rate as your ordinary income (e.g., wage income).

When thinking about the timing of the sale of an investment take into consideration how long you've held the investment. If you're close to the long-term holding period and the sale doesn't have to be done today, wait until the capital gain on the asset is treated as a long-term gain. This will save you money.

Commissions and fees are part of the transaction costs of buying and selling financial assets. We advocate purchasing financial assets either through mutual funds or exchange traded funds (ETFs). A rundown of mutual fund transaction costs includes management fees, distribution fees, redemption fees, reinvestment fees, and exchange fees. These costs reduce return.

OTHER FACTORS

Many other factors influence financial returns: liquidity, interest rates, marketability, government policies, and leverage. Liquidity refers to the ease of converting an asset to money. Money is 100 percent liquid. Suppose you have two assets in your portfolio: a share of Intel stock worth $14 and a house worth $132,000. What we mean by "worth" is its market value. In a matter of minutes, you could sell your share of Intel stock for an amount close to its market value. Can we say the same thing about your house? Selling it at its market value is going to take a few weeks or longer. This makes your house less liquid than your share of Intel stock. Because liquidity is something that investors' desire, they'll accept lower returns in exchange for it.

Changes in interest rates affect prices of financial assets. When interest rates rise, stock and bond prices normally drop and vice versa. Suppose that a two-year treasury bond has a current yield of 2 percent. Interest rates on other debt instruments rise. How will this event affect investor behavior? Everyone will want to sell their two-year treasury bonds and buy these new investments. This causes two-year treasury bond prices to drop.

Marketability refers to the number of buyers and sellers that exist for a financial asset. Stocks traded on the New York Stock Exchange (NYSE) have high marketability. The NYSE is an auction market where many buyers and sellers compete. This results in stock prices that reflect their market value. In contrast, penny stocks traded in the over the counter market (OTC) have low marketability. The OTC isn't an auction market. This raises the question of whether prices on penny stock reflect their true market value. Investors want marketable assets and are willing to pay for it by accepting lower returns.

Government and Federal Reserve policies have an important effect on financial returns through their respective tax and monetary policies. When government implements higher taxes on dividends and capital gains, then returns on financial assets suffer. The Federal Reserve (or the FED) is a quasi-public institution, created by Congress, responsible for controlling our nation's money supply. Over short periods-of-time, the FED has a large impact on interest rates (and thus asset prices) through changes in monetary policy.

Leverage is when you borrow money to invest. This increases returns when you invest successfully because of the smaller personal investment you make. Two possible ways of leveraging stock investments is through margin buying and short selling. The next chapter discusses both these methods.

10

Stocks

TYPES OF STOCK MARKETS

In the United States, the major stock markets are the New York Stock Exchange (NYSE), the American Stock Exchange (AMEX), and the National Association of Securities Dealers (NASDAQ). Both NYSE and AMEX are located in New York City and are auction markets. Auction markets operate by bringing buyers and sellers together in a single location where they compete against each other. Stock buyers want the lowest possible price while sellers want the highest. NASDAQ isn't an auction market and exists electronically nationwide.

Each of these markets trade stocks of different types of companies. The NYSE lists large, well-established businesses. The AMEX lists medium-size companies. NASDAQ was founded to list smaller, faster growing companies that haven't necessarily shown a profit. Over time, however, some NASDAQ companies have grown large and have remained NASDAQ listed (e.g., Dell Computer).

STOCK MARKET INDICES

Stock market indices are tracked daily to capture the overall movement (up and down) of a group of stocks. The most watched stock index in the United States is the Dow Jones Industrial Average (DJIA). This index consists of thirty of America's most important industrial companies. Other important indices are Standard and Poor's 500 (S&P 500) which includes

Chapter 10

mostly industrial but also some transportation, utilities, and financial companies; the NASDAQ Composite Index (NASDAQ) which follows the NASDAQ Stock Market; and the Wilshire 5000 that today has fewer than 5,000 different companies.

The significance of these indices for individual investors is that they provide opportunities to invest inexpensively in large swathes of the American economy through index mutual funds. Chapter 12 has a general discussion of mutual fund investing.

READING STOCK MARKET TABLES

The following is a mock-up of a typical stock market table:

Table 10.1.   Stock Market Table

| Week | | | | | Yld | | Vol | | | | |
Hi	Lo	Stock	Sym	Div	%	PE	100s	Hi	Lo	Close	Net Ch.
22.13	17.75	Fin-Ed	FE	.40	2%	30	680	20.25	19	20	0.75

Begin with the columns labeled "52 Weeks." This refers to the past year. "Hi" and "Lo" references the high and low prices a stock has achieved over the past year. Here, the stock we're examining had a high price of $22.13 and a low price of $17.75. The company that issued this stock is "Fin-Ed" and its ticker symbol is "FE."

FE's estimated next dividend is 0.40—that is, forty cents—per share, which when divided by FE's closing stock price yesterday of $20 per share—look at the "Close" column—generates a (dividend) yield of 2 percent.

FE's price earnings ratio (i.e., PE) equals thirty. Thus, FE's ratio of stock price earnings per share is thirty. Traded yesterday were 680 lots of one hundred shares each of FE stock. This translates into sixty-eight thousand shares of FE trading hands.

Yesterday's high and low price for FE was $20.25 and $19 and, as already stated, FE closed at $20 per share. Finally, between yesterday and the day before yesterday, FE increased in value by $.75.

EVALUATING COMPANY STOCK

Risk and Return

Two variables analyzed when evaluating a company's stock are return and risk. Return on a stock includes dividends and capital appreciation.

If you want to build wealth, capital appreciation should be your primary focus. If you want income, dividends are more important. Publicly traded companies publish their history of dividend payments, growth, and capital appreciation.

One common source for this information is *Value Line* carried by many public libraries. In stock and all other forms of investing, savers search for high returns and low risk.

PE and PD Ratios

Two financial ratios reported in the financial press are PE and PD ratios. PE refers to a stock's price earnings ratio. To calculate PE take a stock's market value and divide it by its earnings per share.

(Price of Stock) ÷ (Earnings Per Share) = PE Ratio

Earnings per share states how much profit each share of stock generates. Effectively, a stock's PE ratio is the cost of buying a slice of a company's future profit. The higher this ratio becomes the less attractive the stock.

Assumed for each industry is a normal PE level. Unfortunately, normality is often hard to evaluate. During the late 1990s, some investors considered Internet stock PE levels to be at astronomical levels while others thought they were about right. Which group was correct? It turned out that Internet stocks were overvalued and by the year 2000, their prices crashed.

PD or price dividend ratio takes the current price of a share of stock and divides it by the stock's dividend payout.

(Stock Market Value) ÷ (Stock's Dividend Payout) = PD Ratio

The PD ratio measures the price you pay for future dividends.

BUYING STOCK ON MARGIN

When you buy stock on margin, you receive a loan from your broker to pay for part of its cost. This loan has an interest charge you must pay as long as the loan is outstanding. The stock you buy acts as collateral against the loan.

The benefit of buying stock on margin is that you can buy more shares than if you use your own money. If the price of the stock you buy rises, you sell your stock, pay back your loan, and pocket the rest. This leads to a higher rate of return than if you invested only your own money.

Of course, the opposite can occur: your stock's price can decline. Now, not only are you losing money on your stock, but you also have to keep paying your broker interest on your margin loan. If your stock's price drops too much, it may no longer act as sufficient collateral and your broker will ask you to put up additional money. This is a margin call. If you can't meet a margin call, your broker liquidates (i.e., sells) your stock and recovers the money lent you.

We don't promote margin buying. Margin buying is too close to gambling to advocate as a savings strategy.

SHORT SELLING

Short selling is the other side of margin buying. When you buy stock on margin, you're betting its price will rise. This is taking a long position. In short selling, you expect the stock you're shorting to drop in price. Short selling is a way to make money when a stock's price goes down.

When you short sell a stock, you borrow shares of the stock from your broker and sell them at their current market value. This generates cash for you. You're expecting the price of the stock to go down in the future. When this happens, you buy the stock back at its lower price and return the shares you borrowed. The profit you earn is the difference between what you sold the stock for originally and the lower cost of buying it back. Again, by using borrowed stock you increase your return if you're successful.

When your broker gives you stock to sell, it's counted as a loan and you must pay interest on it. Now assume that the price of the stock you're shorting rises in price. What then? Now, not only must you continue to pay interest on your loan, but to liquidate (i.e., payback) your position, you must buy this stock back at a cost greater than the cash you received when you sold it.

Our advice is to avoid short selling. It's also more of a gamble than an investment strategy.

11

+

Bonds

Bonds are equally complex an asset to invest in as stocks. Bonds not only come in different varieties, they also have a rating system that measures their risk. Like stocks, bonds have their own published tables that provide investment information.

BOND TERMS

Principal (face value) is a bond's value at its maturity date. The maturity date is the year the borrower will re-pay your investment. Many bonds have a face value of $1,000. The interest paid on a bond is its coupon payment. Most bonds pay interest bi-annually or every six months. Although bonds generally carry less risk than stock, remember that there is an inverse relationship between bond prices and interest rates. If interest rates go up then bond prices of previously issued bonds go down and vice-a-versa.

BOND RATINGS

The best-known bond rating services are Standard and Poor's and Moody's. They rate bonds based on the underlying "financials" of the bond issuer. These "financials" involve various measures of the capacity of the bond issuer to pay back their loans.

Table 11.1.   Standard and Poor's Rating System.

Rating Key	Explanation
AAA	Best quality, smallest risk
AA	High quality, low risk
A	High to medium quality, vulnerable to changing economic conditions
BBB	Medium quality, adequate in terms of safety
BB	Somewhat speculative, moderate safety, not well secured
B	Can currently pay debt but subject to future default risk
CCC	Poor quality and in danger of default
CC	Highly speculative and often in a default state
C	Poor prospects of being paid though may still be paying
D	In default

Talbe 11.2. **How to Read a Bond Quote.**

	Coupon	Maturity Date	Bid Price	Yield		
XYZ Co.	8.25	Oct. 16/25	115.5	6.38		
↑	↑	↑	↑	↑		
column 1	column 2	column 3	column 4	column 5		

As an investor, you need to know that bonds rated BBB or higher are considered investment grade, while bonds rated BB or less are considered junk or non-investment grade. Avoid bonds rated below BBB. Just like stock investing, when buying a bond a decision has to be made between risk and return. As you move from AAA down the quality rating returns go up but so does risk.

Reading a Bond Table

Let's take a look at the bond table, and see how to break it down.

Column 1: Issuer. This is the company, state, province or country that is issuing the bond.

Column 2: Coupon. The coupon refers to the fixed interest rate that the issuer pays to the lender. The coupon rate varies by bond.

Column 3: Maturity Date. This is the date when the borrower will pay the principal back to the lenders (investors). Typically, only the last two digits of the year are quoted, so 25 stands for the year 2025, 04 is 2004, et cetera.

Column 4: Bid Price. This is the price that someone is willing to pay for the bond. It is quoted in relation to 100, regardless of the par value. Think of the bond price as a percentage, a bond with a bid of $93 means it is trading at 93 percent of its par value.

Column 5: Yield. The yield is calculated by the amount of interest paid on a bond divided by its current price—it is a measure of the income generated by a bond.

If the bond is callable it will have a "c" followed by the year in which the bond can be called. For example, c10 means the bond can be called as early as 2010.

12

Mutual Funds

WHAT IS A MUTUAL FUND?

A mutual fund pools individual investors' money into a single fund. The fund then invests in different types of financial assets depending on the mutual fund's objectives. A major advantage of mutual fund investing is that it achieves diversification inexpensively. Diversification reduces risk.

To build a diversified portfolio made up of individual stocks, you would typically need twenty to thirty individual companies to invest in and tens of thousands of dollars. The typical mutual fund invests in hundreds of companies. Best of all you can begin investing in a mutual fund with just a couple of thousand of dollars or less. In some cases, waived is this minimum investment requirement if you set up what is call an automatic account builder. This strategy is also a way of utilizing dollar cost averaging that we discuss later.

Every managed mutual fund has a manager and a team of analysts whose function is to invest their fund's assets. Most of us are fully employed either at work or home and don't have the time or expertise to analyze individual investment opportunities. A managed fund does this for us. There's a charge for this professional management service that is listed as a management fee on a mutual fund prospectus.

FOUR TYPES OF MUTUAL FUNDS

Mutual funds come in different flavors. Experts commonly use the following four-way classification scheme to categorize them:

- Money Market Funds
- Bond Funds
- Balanced Funds
- Stock Funds

Money Market Funds

A money market fund works like a savings account at a bank: every dollar you invest earns interest. One difference between them is that individual savings accounts are insured. Given the types of financial assets money market funds invest in, they're considered essentially risk-free from default.

Money market funds typically pay a higher interest rate than a savings account and they allow check writing. Normally, these checks have some minimum such as $250. Many investors use their money market fund for a place to park their emergency fund to pay for large and unexpected outlays like a major car or home repair.

Earlier, we spoke about cash equivalent assets. Money market mutual funds invest in cash equivalent assets such as treasury bills (T-bills), commercial paper, and short-term municipal bonds.

Money market mutual funds are either taxable or tax-free. Taxable funds buy the highest yielding short-term corporate and government debt issues available. Tax-free funds are limited to buying municipal debt. Taxable funds pay higher interest rates but investors must pay taxes on this income. Roughly, either of these fund types will pay what a bank pays on its money market accounts or CDs without forcing you to commit your money for a predetermined time.

Bond Funds

The purpose of bond funds is mostly to produce income as opposed to capital appreciation. (There are junk bond funds that invest in high-risk instruments that try to achieve capital appreciation.)

Two differences between a bond mutual fund and purchasing bonds individually are that bond funds have no maturity date and make no repayment guarantee. If you purchase a thirty-year treasury bond, you know that in thirty years you'll receive its par value. If you put the same amount of money in a bond mutual fund, even one that invests in treasury bonds, after thirty years your investment might be worth less than its original value. This is why some investment counselors recommend that bond investors invest directly in individual bonds as opposed to buying a bond mutual fund.

However, bond mutual funds have two advantages over purchasing bonds directly. First, for a relatively small amount of money, you can buy into a diversified bond mutual fund. Creating a diversified bond portfolio on your own is expensive and not feasible for the average investor. Second, bond funds allow you the opportunity to reinvest bond coupon payments into the fund where you can purchase additional fund shares.

Different types of bond funds exist. As an investor, you have to make three decisions concerning bond mutual funds: level of risk exposure, short- or long-term maturity, and taxable or tax-free.

The least risky bond funds invest in treasury bonds. Three types of treasury securities exist: T-bills, notes, and bonds. T-bills mature in less than one year; notes mature from one to ten years; and bonds for ten to thirty years. At the other end of the risk spectrum are the junk bond funds that have a higher chance of defaulting. As savers and investors, we recommend that investors seek professional advice before investing in junk securities.

Bond funds invest in bonds of different maturities. Three lengths of maturity for bond funds are short-term, which is less than three years; medium-term, three to ten years; and long-term, greater than ten years. The longer the term of the bond fund the greater its risk and the greater its return. The length of time you select to invest depends on your goals and your expectations whether interest rates are going up or down. The further away a bond's maturity date the greater its price fluctuation in response to interest rate changes. If your child is five years away from attending college, don't invest their college money in a thirty-year bond. Rising interest rates depress thirty-year bond prices by a larger amount than five-year bond prices. If interest rates are high and you're a long-term investor, you might want to lock in these high rates in with a thirty-year bond.

Similar to money market mutual funds, bond funds come in taxable and tax-free versions. Income earned on corporate, treasury, and federal agency bonds must pay federal income taxes. Earnings from treasury bonds don't pay state and local taxes while municipal bonds don't pay federal income taxes.

If you purchase municipal bonds from the state or municipality where you reside in you don't pay state or local taxes. For example, New Yorkers can buy triple tax-free municipal bonds and keep all of their earnings.

Your choice to invest in a taxable or tax-free bond depends on their yield difference and your tax bracket. Tax-free bonds always carry lower yields than taxable bonds. Depending on your tax bracket, a municipal bond might not be your best investment. Below is the formula for calculating tax equivalent yields. This formula converts the return on a tax-free bond into its taxable equivalent.

Tax-free Coupon Yield ÷ (1 – Tax Bracket) = Tax Equivalent Yield

Assume that your choice is between a corporate bond that has a yield of 8 percent (taxable) and a municipal bond with a yield of 6 percent (tax-free). Which would you choose? Say that you're in the 28 percent tax bracket.

Following this formula, divide 6 percent by 72 percent (1 – 28 percent). This equals 8.33 percent. This means that our 6 percent municipal bond is equivalent to an 8.33 percent corporate bond. Here you would opt for the municipal security. Notice that the greater your tax bracket, the more attractive municipal bonds become.

Balanced Funds

Balanced funds invest in stocks and bonds—this is why they are considered "balanced." The goal of balanced funds is income and growth. Balanced funds are appropriate for intermediate-term investing and carry moderate risk. Many investors like the fact that in a single fund they can own both stocks and bonds. When stock prices are rising this type of fund will also go up, just not as much as a fund that invests only in stocks. During stock market declines, balanced funds will have a better return than all stock funds because the bond portion of the fund will help minimize its losses, since there is an income stream that is generated by its bond holdings.

There are different levels of risk in bond funds based on the type of bonds the fund invests. A high-grade corporate bond fund will be less aggressive than a high yield (junk bond) fund, but more aggressive than a government bond fund.

Stock Funds

Stock funds invest in stock. The major distinction among stock funds is between those that pursue income (i.e., dividends) and those that pursue growth (i.e., capital appreciation). Some stock funds seek both. Normally, stock funds that invest for income are less risky than those that invest for capital appreciation. Regardless of the goals of the fund, you must pay taxes on fund profits when you sell your stock fund shares.

Like bond funds, there are different levels of risk an investor can take with stock funds. An aggressive growth (invests in smaller companies)

fund will be investing in far more risky companies than a large cap income fund (invests in established companies that pay a dividend).

For every type of investor, there is a mutual fund to match their level of risk and investment interest. Below is a partial, but important, list of stock fund types:

- Blue chip funds invest in well-established companies. Their major goal is income.
- Growth funds invest in companies that show profit growth. Their goal is capital appreciation.
- Cyclical funds invest in companies whose profit is sensitive to economic expansions and recessions. Cyclical funds are a way of combating risk linked to the business cycle.
- Value funds invest in undervalued companies. The goal of value funds is capital appreciation.

Special Purpose Funds

Among special purpose funds, the two that are most important for individual investors are stock index and tax-free funds. Two other fund types described are sector funds and green funds.

- Index funds give you the return earned on a basket of stocks (or bonds) that comprise an index such as the Standard and Poor's 500. Other well-known indices are the Wilshire 5000, the Russell 2000, the Dow Jones 30, and the NASDAQ Composite. These index funds have become very popular because their performance, on average, has surpassed what managed funds achieve. Managed mutual funds pay professional managers to select investments. The mutual fund's investors pay these professionals. Index funds don't have portfolio managers that actively manage the fund.
- Index funds buy into a selection of securities based on the goals of the fund. When the overall prices, weighted by number of shares, of the stocks that the fund purchased rise, the fund's share price rises and vice versa. What's surprising is that these index funds often outperform professionally managed funds—there's an economic theory to explain this fact. In addition, managed funds are more expensive to own. This is why many mutual fund investors have abandoned managed funds in favor of index funds.
- Sector funds invest in a sector (or part) of the economy such as technology, energy, financial services, and health care. In some sense, sector funds violate our belief in diversification. While sector funds achieve diversity within an economic sector, they lack overall

diversity. Consequently, sector funds are more volatile and display greater risk. One benefit of sector funds is that they allow you to achieve diversity inexpensively within an economic sector. For example, you believe that out of the many healthcare companies that currently exist, only a few are going to be profitable in the future. However, you don't know which ones are going to be future winners. One way of surmounting this difficulty is to purchase a sector fund that specializes in health care companies. This is like placing bets on all horses that run a particular race. If the overall health care sector does well, you'll make money. While this has the aura of gambling to it, there are circumstances where sector funds are an appropriate investment.

- Tax-free funds are funds whose distributions are at least partly free of taxes. The beneficiaries of tax-free funds are investors who live in high tax states and are in a high tax bracket. For example, California is a high tax state. Assume that you're a resident of California and you're in a high tax bracket. By buying a tax-free fund that specializes in California municipal bonds, you can avoid both federal and state taxes on earned income.

- Green funds invest in companies that make "concerned" environmental decisions and display political and social consciousness. Such funds wouldn't invest in tobacco companies or in countries that have repressive political regimes. The general belief is that Green funds have a lower level of return than funds that are free to invest in any type of company.

International Funds

A well-diversified personal portfolio should contain international investments. Because business cycle movements across economies differ, investing internationally reduces risk. There are periods when the Japanese economy is doing well while the US economy isn't. This might translate into a "bullish" Japanese stock market and a "bearish" US stock market. "Bullish" means that investors believe stock prices will rise; "bearish" means that investors believe that stock prices will fall.

An additional reason to invest in international funds is that different economies grow at different rates. Take the examples of China and Brazil. Up to recently, both of these economies were growing more rapidly than the US economy. This translates into greater corporate profits for Chinese and Brazilian companies and faster appreciating stock values.

The easiest way of internationalizing your portfolio is through international mutual funds. Knowing how to read their labels will prevent you from making wrong investment choices.

- International funds invest in foreign stocks and bonds.
- Global funds invest in both United States and international stocks and bonds.
- Regional funds invest in particular geographic regions such as Latin America, Europe, and the Pacific Rim.
- Country funds invest in particular countries such as Japan, Germany, et cetera.

For purposes of diversification, we recommend an international fund. International funds invest worldwide and thus achieve diversification. The problem with global funds is that they invest heavily in US securities. If you're already invested in US assets, why further invest in them? Regional and country funds carry greater risks and the possibility of greater returns.

Exchange Traded Funds (ETFs)

ETFs are a type of investment fund that includes anywhere from a dozen companies to several thousand. Where they differ from a regular mutual fund is in their pricing. The price of a mutual fund's share is set at the end of a trading day. ETFs trade like a single share of stock. During a trading day, their price fluctuates. This gives investors the opportunity to trade their ETFs like individual shares of stock.

You can also place a stop-loss order on an ETF, something you can't do with a mutual fund. (A stop loss order instructs your broker to sell your ETF when the price drops to a certain point. Its purpose is to minimize your losses.)

ETFs have become more popular with average investors. Today there are over a thousand ETFs to choose from and they cover the full range of investment risk and return. Like mutual funds, there is a type of ETF to match every type of investor and financial goal.

Two big advantages of ETFs are that they trade like individual shares of stock and their low management fees. Two significant disadvantages of ETFs are your need to have a brokerage account to buy and sell them and their transaction fees—every time you buy and sell an ETF you must pay a fee.

We have mixed feeling about using ETFs as part of a long-term, dollar cost investment strategy. The fact that they trade like individual shares of stock is a plus from our calculus. However, their transaction fees, long-term, can really eat into your wealth accumulation. Some evidence is mounting that ETF transaction fees are declining and may disappear in the future. If this happens, the attractiveness of ETFs relative to standard mutual funds will rise significantly.

MEASURING A MUTUAL FUND'S PERFORMANCE

When you invest in a mutual fund, you purchase shares in that fund. The price of an individual share is its net asset value or NAV calculated using this formula:

Value of Fund ÷ Number of Fund Shares = NAV

The value of the fund is the fund's market value in dollars. The number of fund shares outstanding is self-explanatory. For NAV to increase, the fund's value must rise.

Suppose that the value of some fund equals $1,000,000 and its number of outstanding shares is 1,000. What's NAV? The answer is $1,000

The total return of holding a mutual fund share equals:

$$[(D_t + NAV_{END} - NAV_{START}) \div NAV_{START}] \times 100\%$$

D_t is distributions you have received from the mutual fund company (e.g., dividends, interest, capital gains) per share. NAV_{END} is the ending value of one mutual fund share and NAV_{START} is the price you initially paid for a share.

As an illustration, five years ago you purchased a mutual fund share for $500. Today it's worth $1250. Over the five years you received various distributions totaling $75. What's your total return?

$$[(\$75 + \$1250 - \$500) \div \$500] \times 100\% = 165\%$$

READING MUTUAL FUND QUOTATIONS

Earlier we looked at stock and bond tables. Mutual funds have their own table listing in newspapers. Here we explain how to read a mutual fund quotation. Financial newspapers, such as the Wall Street Journal, have very thorough guides that can help you interpret the small print found in mutual fund tables.

Look at the table below.

Table 12.1. Mutual Fund Table

Name of Company	Investment Objective	NAV	Offer Price	NAV Change	YTD	1 yr	3 yrs	Relative Ranking
Fin-Ed p	GRO	10.71	11.23	-0.05	+8.2	+7.1	+12.7	A

Fin-Ed is the name of the mutual fund. The lowercase "p" after the fund's name describes a type of fee fund holders must pay. Here it stands for 12b-1 fees. Other letters used after a mutual fund's name includes "r" which stands for back-end load fees and "t" which means both "r" and "p" applies. We'll discuss these later.

GRO stands for Fin-Ed's investment objective of growth. Other objectives you'll read in mutual fund tables are capital appreciation (CAP); growth and income (G&I); equity income (EQI); and sector fund (SEC).

A NAV of 10.71 stands for $10.71. The offer price ($11.23) is what you pay to purchase more fund shares. Its offer price is greater than its NAV because Fin-Ed is charging a load or commission to buy its shares. In this example, the load equals $0.52 per share.

NAV change is the difference between yesterday's closing NAV and the day before. In this example, NAV declined by 5 percent. The +8.2 or +8.2 percent is the yield to date (YTD) return earned on a Fin-Ed share from the beginning of the year to today. YTD assumes you reinvest all distributions.

Over the last fifty-two weeks, Fin-Ed shares returned 7.1 percent and over the last three years, 12.7 percent. The *A* in the last column represents the relative ranking of Fin-Ed among funds like itself. An *A* means that Fin-Ed was in the top 20 percent of funds similar to itself. These letters run down to *E*, which represents the bottom 20 percent.

MUTUAL FUND RETURN AND RISK

Every mutual fund carries some measure of return and risk. Below is a table with an ordinal ranking of risk and return for different types of mutual funds. (Ordinal means that we can say that one number is greater than another but not by how much.)

Taable 12.2.   Mutual Fund Return and Risk

Types of Mutual fund	Investment Types	Risk Level	Return Level	Investment Period
Money Market	Cash Equivalents	1	1	0 to +years
Bond	Debt Instruments	2	2	3 to 9 years
Balance Fund	Debt and Equity	3	3	7 to 10 years
Stock	Equity	4	4	10+ years

Money market mutual funds have the lowest return and are the least risky. Money market funds are places to "park" cash assets for purposes of writing large checks and to maintain an emergency fund. Money market mutual funds have no minimum timeframe.

Bond funds carry more risk than money market funds and generate greater returns. The purpose of a bond fund is to generate income. When interest rates rise, the value of bond fund shares goes down and vice versa. Long-term bond funds (holds bonds with greater than ten year maturities) are more sensitive to changes in interest rates than short or intermediate-term bond funds. When interest rates are expected to rise, don't invest in a long-term bond fund—its value will fall more than a short- or intermediate-term fund. If you expect interest rates to fall, then a long-term fund can be an attractive investment because you can lock in high interest rates.

If you're saving for a goal that is five years away, investing in an intermediate bond fund is appropriate. If your savings goal is seven to ten years out, it makes sense to have a balanced fund that contains both bonds and stocks because you want both income and capital appreciation. Finally, if your savings goal is more than ten years away, consider moving toward a more heavily weighted stock fund.

In the above discussion, we never mention the purpose of any savings goal. Not always, but often, purpose is unimportant. A person is sixty-five years old and expects to live another ten years. A family is saving for a child's college education that is ten years away. The sixty-five-year-old should invest to generate both income to live on and capital appreciation if he or she lives longer than ten years. Our family wants to be confident that the money they save will be there in ten years. A college savings program also requires capital appreciation to help pay the cost of college. The investments that are appropriate for both situations might be very similar.

READING A MUTUAL FUND PROSPECTUS

Reading a mutual fund prospectus is one of the more tedious aspects of mutual fund investing. A prospectus is designed to tell you a fund's goal and fees. While it's possible to invest in a more popular mutual fund without bothering to read the fund's small print, we encourage everybody to read the prospectus of any mutual fund being considered as an investment. In fact, when talking with a mutual fund representative he or she is required to ask if you have read the prospectus and agree to its terms and conditions before opening an account for you.

Below is a list of the important items to understand when reading a mutual fund's prospectus:

- Statement of objective
- Fund fees and expenses
- Fund performance
- Shareholder services

Statement of Objective

Two common mutual fund objectives are growth and income. Some funds—balanced funds—combine both goals. If you're young and saving for retirement then you should invest for growth. As you become older, income becomes more important. Developing your own mutual fund portfolio is more a question of blending growth with income than opting for one over the other.

Fund Fees and Expenses

Smart investors avoid fees and taxes. Basic fees discussed in a mutual fund prospectus are management fees, distribution or 12b-1 fees, redemption fees, deferred sales load, reinvestment fees, and exchange fees. Managed funds have higher management fees than index funds. Management fees normally run 0.5 percent to 2 percent of assets under management. Distribution fees pay for the funds marketing. Many funds don't charge a distribution fee. Redemption fees occur when you sell your fund's shares. Partly, redemption fees are designed to encourage investors to keep their money invested and discourage what's called in-and-out-trading. Reinvestment fees happen when you reinvest fund distributions. Finally, exchange fees apply when you move money from one mutual fund to another within the same mutual fund company. Mutual fund magazines often compress many of these payments into the categories of front and back load fees. This describes where in the purchase of a mutual fund you pay these costs. Front load means that there are fees to get into the mutual fund while back load refers to fees you must pay to get out of the mutual fund.

Another common fee-based distinction is between load and no-load funds. Load means the fund has a sales charge. This charge may occur at the time of the purchase, at redemption, or both. No-load means there's no sales charge going in or out of the fund. Some funds are no-load if the money remains invested for a minimum amount of time.

As an investor, it's important to account for all of these fees and compare them to the long-term return the fund has achieved. If a fund with greater fees has greater long-term performance, it can make sense to invest in it. Our experience, though, is when looking at a fund with many fees but good solid long-term performance, one can always find a less expensive counterpart that does just as well.

Fund Performance

Evaluating the performance of a mutual fund can be tricky. Like any investment, you must look at a fund's return and risk. Often, mutual funds that did well the previous year emphasize that year's performance. A single year's performance will not show enough information to make an educated decision about a fund. A funds performance over a ten-year period will give you a good picture as to how it will perform in both good and bad times. Most ten-year periods include a bull and bear market. For us, this really establishes a fund's record of accomplishment.

When researching mutual fund performance most fund families will list each of their fund's performance in terms year to date (January 1 to the day you look it up), one year (going back twelve months from today), three, five, and ten years. They may also provide the return since the fund has started and this figure made go all the way back to 1930s or 1940s.

In evaluating a fund's performance, always look as far back as possible. Nevertheless, even evidence of good performance over one decade does not insure its continuance over the next decade. Twentieth Century Growth was the number one ranked equity fund in the decade of the 1970s. In the decade of the 1980s, it fell to 176. The number two fund in the 1970s, Templeton Growth, went from number 2 to 126 in the 1980s. Many examples like this exist. Humans manage mutual funds. Human strategies often fit particular investment periods. What works today might not work tomorrow.

Another factor that will affect fund performance is the fund's manager. The objectives of the fund will guide the fund manager, but he or she will make the final decision as to which companies to buy. The only exception to this is an index fund. There is research that argues that index funds tend to outperform many actively managed funds.

Shareholder Services

Shareholder services refer to investment options, reinvestment options, exchange services, redemption options, and check writing privileges. Investment options deal with the various ways you can buy and sell your fund shares—by phone, mail, e-mail, et cetera. Electronic funds transfer is one convenient way of sending money from your bank to a mutual fund company. This feature gives you the opportunity to transfer money without having to write a check or even make a call. An investor decides how much to invest each month and its transfer date to the mutual fund company. The mutual fund company will then automatically buy additional shares.

Reinvestment options determine the various ways you can manage your distributions. Exchange services describe your ability to move money from one mutual fund to another. Mutual fund companies often offer their customers different types of mutual funds. Redemption options tell you the ways you can obtain your money. They include checks, electronic transfers, and automatic withdrawal plans. As discussed earlier, check writing is most important when investing in a money market mutual fund.

HOW TO PURCHASE MUTUAL FUNDS

One common misunderstanding is that you must use a third party like an investment company to purchase shares in a mutual fund. Many ways of buying mutual fund shares exist. The method we recommend is to buy directly from mutual fund companies. You can call any mutual fund company and ask them to send you a prospectus on any fund. All mutual fund companies have their own web site where you can request a prospectus or buy directly into the fund. If you buy a mutual fund through an intermediary such as a bank, broker, or other financial agent, they're going to charge a fee. Also, be careful of financial advice from these sources. Sometimes, they only recommend funds that their company owns or where they earn the highest commissions.

13

✛

Portfolio Design

FACTORS THAT AFFECT YOUR PORTFOLIO MIX

How to allocate your savings between stocks, bonds, and cash assets is your portfolio decision. In the savings and investment process, many investment experts consider this the most critical choice you make.

Most investors believe that the secret to earning high returns is "picking the right individual stock." However, empirical evidence suggests that having a correct asset allocation between stocks, bonds, and cash assets ultimately determines your financial returns. How you invest in any one of these particular categories seems less important. Your asset allocation should fit your needs and tolerance for risk.

As stated in chapter 1, we distinguish between investing and gambling by always linking an investment strategy with a savings goal. Investing doesn't take place in a vacuum. Your savings goals affect your investment strategies by dictating your targeted dollar amount and timeframe. Other factors affecting your portfolio decision include your risk attitude and investment time horizon.

Targeted Dollar Amounts

The more money, income, or wealth you want in the future, the more you must save and/or expose yourself to greater risk. Greater risk means holding most of your portfolio in stock. To reach any financial goal, there's a trade-off between the amount you save and your risk exposure. If you want to save less, the more you must commit to investing in stocks and the greater your risk exposure. If you're willing to save more, you can hold more of your portfolio in the form of bonds and cash assets and thus reduce your risk exposure.

Timeframe

The longer you stay invested, the more your portfolio should contain stock. Given enough—we like ten plus years—the risk associated with a well-diversified stock portfolio begins to look like the risk associated with holding debt instruments and cash assets. If your savings timeframe is less than five years, then your portfolio should be limited to cash assets and maybe short-term bonds. Intermediate timeframes tend to dictate portfolios that have more of a mix of stocks, bonds, and cash assets.

Risk Attitudes

Three attitudes toward risk are risk lover, risk averse, and risk neutral. We assume no one reading our book is a risk lover when it comes to investing. Risk lovers are people who are willing to pay to be exposed to risk. Most of us, when it comes to personal investing, are risk averse. If you're risk averse then you require a premium to take on risk. Stocks are riskier than bonds and, therefore, carry higher returns. A person who is risk neutral simply ignores risk.

The greater your risk aversion, the more your portfolio should contain bonds and cash assets. The less your risk aversion, the more your portfolio should contain stock. Each investor needs to be comfortable with the investment choices they make.

Go to this link to help you think about your risk tolerance: money.usnews. com/money/blogs/the-smarter-mutual-fund-investor/2013/04/02/ whats-your-risk-tolerance.

Dollar Cost Averaging

Dollar cost averaging is an investment strategy that is easy to implement and powerful in building wealth. In dollar cost averaging, no matter how financial markets are performing, a fixed schedule of saving and investing is followed.

Earlier you developed your set of goals and determined how much money you needed to reach each goal on a monthly basis. We recommend setting up an automatic investment plan for each goal or group of goals based on dollar cost averaging. This strategy has worked for many people in reaching their financial goals. In addition, it doesn't require a lot of money to begin.

The logic behind dollar cost averaging is the assumption that "turning points" aren't predictable. Turning points occur when financial markets go from rising to falling values and vice versa. We believe that nobody can forecast this consistently. If you could predict turning points, then you would buy into financial markets when they had a low value and sell when they had a high value. Dollar cost averaging is for savers and investors who can't do this. (Again, our view is that no investor can consistently predict turning points.)

The dollar cost averaging method involves investing a constant dollar amount (e.g., $100) at regular intervals (e.g., every paycheck). What occurs when you use this method is that when financial markets are doing well, you purchase fewer shares—assuming we're talking about mutual fund investing—and when financial markets are doing poorly, then you buy more shares. This is exactly what you want to accomplish as an investor. When financial assets are "cheap," you want to buy a lot of them and where they're "expensive," you want to buy few of them.

EXAMPLES OF ASSET ALLOCATIONS

The Conservative Investor

Conservative investors exhibit greater risk aversions. Being conservative can be a result of age, the types of goals pursued, the length of time invested, et cetera. Normally, when we talk about a conservative portfolio we mean one that has more cash assets and intermediate-term bonds in it. No "fast and fixed" rules exist for defining the exact nature of a conservative portfolio. Figure 13.1 illustrates one of the many asset allocations that can satisfy the definition of conservative.

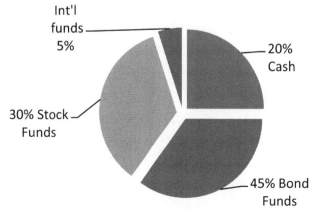

Figure 13.1.   Asset Allocation for a Conservative Investor

Moderate Investor

This type of portfolio will preserve wealth and interest income with some capital appreciation.

Relative to the conservative investor, the moderate investor shows greater tolerance for risk. This infers a portfolio with more stock investments. Again, what causes an investor to exhibit moderation in their investing includes factors such as age, savings goals pursued, length of time invested, and so forth. Again, no fixed definition of a moderate portfolio exists. The asset allocation we show in figure 13.2 is just one of many possibilities.

This portfolio is 65 percent invested in stock divided between the United States and the rest of the world, moderately invested in bonds, and lightly invested in cash assets. More of the earnings of this portfolio will be in the form of stock dividends and capital appreciation.

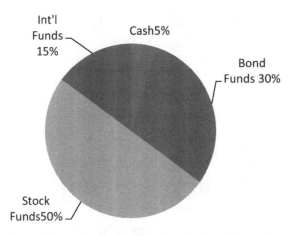

Figure 13.2.   Asset Allocation for a Moderate Investor.

Aggressive Investor

Everything said about the conservative and moderate investor holds for the aggressive investor. Don't interpret the word aggressive to mean gambling. We think anyone who is twenty years old and is saving for retirement should be an aggressive investor.

What makes the portfolio described in figure 13.3 aggressive is its 80 percent allocation in stock. This portfolio will earn a lot of dividend income and capital appreciation. Long-term, stock investments are the best way to build wealth.

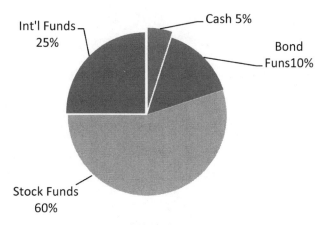

Figure 13.3.   Asset Allocation for an Aggressive Investor

14

Three Explicit Examples of Investment Problems

THE RETIREMENT PROBLEM

The purpose of retirement planning is to have sufficient income to live when you stop working. Retirees, until recently, were somewhat assured that between Social Security and company pensions, their future income needs would be met. This is no longer true. Social Security's future is cloudy and businesses for the most part have  stopped offering defined-benefit plans. This leaves the average person with the need to plan for his or her own retirement.

Whatever your age, retirement planning requires that you begin by asking and answering the following questions.

When do I want to retire?

This is your call. The further in the future your retirement date, the easier it is to accumulate wealth. We see the idea of retirement becoming passé. When we advise people in their twenties or even early thirties, we emphasize saving for future lifestyle or career changes. Evidence shows that work is healthy for you. We believe that your long-term savings should really be for affording lifestyle changes without having to worry about income.

How much income do I want at retirement?

The best recommendation is that retirees should aim for a yearly retirement income of at least 60 percent to 80 percent of their pre-retirement income. Our personal comfort level is to strive for a higher percentage, try for 100 percent. We advise this because the future is ultimately unknowable. This way, if you fall short there should still be plenty of income to live comfortably. One of us watched his parents become nearly broke during the 1970s because of unexpected inflation. We believe in erring on the side of having too much income rather than too little.

What's my current projected Social Security income?

Earlier we asked you to review your Social Security benefit statement. Again, if you haven't received this statement from Social Security, then contact them and request it. You need the information contained in your summary statement for retirement planning.

What's my current projected income from my employer's retirement plan?

Many Americans work under an employer-sponsored retirement plan. Three types of sponsored plans exist: defined-benefit, defined-contribution, and profit-sharing plans.

In a defined-benefit plan, your employer guarantees a specific dollar amount when you retire based on your length-of-time of employment, salary, et cetera. In a defined-contribution plan, you and (sometimes) your employer contribute toward your retirement. What you collect at retirement depends on plan contributions and how well your chosen investments performed. In a profit-sharing plan, your company, normally out of profit, sets aside money for your retirement.

Find out your plan type and your projected retirement income.

What's the size of my income shortfall?

Subtract from target income what you expect to receive from Social Security and your company's pension plan. Most people have an income shortfall. You must accumulate sufficient financial assets to generate this income shortfall.

Even if you don't have a shortfall, continue to read.

How large of an inheritance do I want to leave my heirs?

Our advice on inheritance is mixed. If you can afford to pass on a wealth legacy to your children and others, then do it. If you're like the average person and you're struggling to get enough income to retire on, ignore inheritance in your retirement plan.

At retirement, what will be the future size of my current wealth held outside my company's retirement plan?

Currently, some part of your wealth might be in the form of your home, private retirement accounts, annuities, et cetera. Calculate their future value at the time of your retirement. Ignore your house in making this calculation. Homes don't generate income unless you do a reverse mortgage or sell it, buy a house of lesser value, and invest the difference.

How much wealth will I need to cover my income shortfall and the inheritance I want to leave?

You must calculate the wealth necessary to cover your income shortfall and your inheritance goal.

What's the difference between the wealth I will need to cover my income shortfall and inheritance goals and the future value of my current wealth held outside my company's retirement program?

Subtract the future value of your current wealth from the wealth you'll need to sustain both your income shortfall and your inheritance goals. This difference is your wealth shortfall. If the number is positive, you're done. If the number is negative, you must develop a retirement savings plan beyond your Social Security and pension.

How much do I have to save to make-up any shortfall in my wealth requirements?

You must now calculate the wealth necessary to cover both your income shortfall and your inheritance goals. Once this is determined, you'll need a savings plan to makeup this shortfall.

Example

Take the case of Pat, a thirty-six-year-old who's single. She wants to retire at age fifty-five and desires to leave an inheritance of $100,000 to her sister's two children. While her current income is $56,000, her best guess is that by the time she retires she will be earning around $95,000.

Upon retirement, Pat expects to have $400,000 in her company's 401 (k) plan. Currently, she owns a condominium that has a market value of $140,000 and an IRA (i.e., individual retirement account) worth $47,000. She thinks of herself as moderately risk averse.

Years to Retirement: nineteen years

Desired Income: $95,000 ($\times$) 100% = $95,000 (She is following our advice and wants to plan to generate 100 percent of her income at retirement.)

Current Projected Social Security Income: $15,000
Income from Company 401(k): $20,000

At retirement, Pat expects to have $400,000 in her company 401(k). Best advice is that during retirement you shouldn't draw down more than 5 percent of your retirement wealth as income each year. This means that Pat can generate at most $20,000 in income per year from her $400,000 ($400,000 $\times$ .05 = $20,000).

Project Retirement Income Shortfall: $60,000

Desired yearly income ($95,000) – Projected yearly Social Security income ($15,000) – Projected income from company 401(k) ($20,000) = $60,000.

Cover Inheritance Target: $25,842

Pat estimates she will live twenty years after retirement. She plans to leave an inheritance at her death. At age fifty-five, she needs sufficient wealth that will grow in twenty years to $100,000. This $25,842 is an estimate of what she'll need to accomplish her inheritance goal assuming a 7 percent yearly return.

NOTE: The above calculation required present value analysis. Go to appendix 1, column 7 percent and row 20. The number in the cell is 3.8697. If you divide $100,000 by this number, it gives you its present value of $25,842. Assuming a return of 7 percent, $25,842 will grow into $100,000 in twenty years.

Future Value of Personal Wealth Excluding Her Work 401(k): $169,976

Pat has two assets: her condominium and her IRA account. If her condominium grows in value 3 percent per year, in nineteen years it will be worth $254,490. (Go to appendix 1, column 3 percent and row 19. The number in the cell is 1.7535. Multiply the present value of her condo, $140,000, by 1.7535 to arrive at its future value of $245,490.)

Her personal IRA in nineteen years, assuming a 7 percent yearly return, will be worth $169,976. (Go to appendix 1, column 7 percent and row 19. The number in the cell is 3.6165. Multiply the present value of pat's IRA, $47,000, by 3.6165 to arrive at its future value.)

For purposes of making sure she has enough income to live on when she retires, Pat should probably ignore the future value of her home. When she retires, she will still need a place to live. She should use the $245,490 to cover her future housing needs. Many people choose to move once they retire. The future value of her condo can be used to purchase a new home in her new location.

Wealth Necessary to Cover Income Shortfalls: $1,200,000

Pat has an income shortfall of $60,000. We calculate this by taking her target income of $95,000 and subtracting her projected Social Security Income of $15,000 and her income from her company's 401(k) of $20,000. To cover $60,000 this shortfall, she needs approximately $1,200,000 in wealth.

NOTE: The above calculation assumes that Pat only takes 5 percent of her wealth each year in the form of income. Dividing her $60,000 shortfall in retirement income by 5 percent tells her that she'll need an additional $1,200,000 in wealth ($60,000 ÷ 0.05 = $1,200,000.).

Projected Shortfall in Wealth: $1,055,866

If Pat adds to wealth necessary to cover her income shortfall ($1,200,000) the additional wealth she needs to cover her inheritance goal ($25,842), and subtract the future value of her personal IRA ($169,976) she has a deficit of wealth equal to $1,055,866.

Develop a Savings Plan

Pat needs to develop an investment plan to cover her wealth shortfall of $1,055,866. Assuming a return of 7 percent, she needs to save around $28,248 additional dollars each year to accumulate her wealth shortfall. (Go to appendix 2, column 7 percent and row 19. The number in the cell is 37.379. Dividing $1,055,866 by 37.379 gives her the yearly required additional savings.)

This amount of required additional savings is probably beyond her means. Pat will have to adjust some combination of her desired retirement income, age of retirement, and inheritance goal to develop a retirement strategy she can afford.

NOTE: In this example we ignored the value of Pat's condo at her death. We also ignore the value of her various retirement accounts at her death. Both of these would more than cover her inheritance goal of $100,000. Building both of these into her planning would reduce her projected wealth shortfall.

Please go through this example multiply times with paper and pencil at hand. Just reading it will not teach you much except the need to commit to paper your financial goals. In this case, Pat learned that her dreams are only possible with, what would be for most people, an additional investment burden that isn't affordable. Better that Pat know this nineteen years before she retires than the day she quits working.

Developing Your Retirement Plan

In this exercise, we're ignoring taxes. You'll need to use the tables in appendices 1 and 2 to develop your retirement plan. Follow Pat's example if you get stuck.

Step 1

Planned Years to Retirement _____

Step 2: Desired Yearly Retirement Income

Projected Average Income during the Last Three Years of Your Work Life:
$_____ ($\times$) (60% to 100%) = $_____

Step 2 requires some guess work. You must project your current income into the future and try to predict how much you'll be earning at the time of your retirement. The older you are, the easier this exercise becomes. If you're at a stage in your life where thinking about retirement income seems too far away, then enter a desired retirement income. The 60 percent to 100 percent multiplier determines the percentage of your working income you want at retirement. We suggest trying for 100 percent and that way, even if you fall a little short of the goal, you should have enough money to live comfortably.

Step 3

Enter Your Projected Social Security Income $_____

Social Security is running out of money. In the future, to keep Social Security solvent, some combination of raising Social Security taxes, delaying the Social Security age and cutting Social Security benefits will have to take place. We encourage people under forty to downplay or just ignore your expected Social Security benefit. This way whatever happens to Social Security will have a minor impact on you.

Step 4

Enter Your Projected Work Retirement Income: $_____

Work retirement income refers to both traditional private or public pensions and 401(k) types of plans. For 401(k) wealth, remember to multiply it by no more than 5 percent to calculate yearly income you can realize.

As an illustration, if you have $400,000 in your 401(k) at retirement then you can take as income no more than $20,000 a year ($400,000 × .05 = $20,000). Again, this advice is based on past history. Drawing down more than 5 percent a year exposes you to the real possibility of being broke, healthy, and old—a terrible combination.

Step 5: Retirement Income Surplus/Shortfall

Desired Income $_____ – Projected Social Security Income $_____ – Projected Company Retirement Income $_____ = Retirement Income Surplus/Shortfall $_____

In Step 8, we assume this number is a shortfall. If the number is a surplus then you're covering your income needs. You still have to plan for your inheritance goals discussed later.

Step 6: Required Inheritance Wealth

If you plan on leaving an inheritance, it's important at retirement to have sufficient wealth to cover all of your inheritance goals. To make this calculation, you need to assume a return you'll be earning on set aside wealth during retirement, have a target age when you plan to give the inheritance and a dollar amount you plan to give. Review Pat's example for additional guidance.

Assumed Rate of Return _____%
Target Age to Give Inheritance – Age at Retirement = _____

Targeted Amount of Inheritance $_____

Now go to appendix 1. Your assumed rate of return determines column and the difference between target age and age at retirement determines row. Divide the number in the cell into targeted amount to determine required inheritance wealth.

Targeted Amount of Inheritance \$_____ ÷ Cell Number _____ =
Required Inheritance Wealth \$_____

The next step estimates how much wealth you'll accumulate through your non-employment investment accounts such as a traditional or Roth IRA. Even though your house is part of your private wealth, in the future you'll need it to live in or use its cash value to purchase another home. For this reason, we ignore its future value.

NOTE: A few things to consider that we're ignoring is first, the possibility of using the value of your home at death to fund your inheritance goals. Second, there are ways to convert home equity into an income stream such as a reverse mortgage. We're ignoring these possibilities. However, you shouldn't.

Step 7: Future Value of Current Non-Employment Investments

Current Value of Non-Employment Investments \$_____ (×) Future Value Multiplier _____ = Future Value of Non-Employment Investments \$_____

To make this calculation you need to know two things: first, how many years until you retire and an assumed rate of return on your investments.

Say that you are twenty years away from retirement and assume you'll earn 7 percent on your investments. Now go to appendix 1, column 7 percent and row 20. The number in the cell is 3.8697. In this example, this number is your Future Value Multiplier.

See Pat's example for additional guidance.

Step 8: Wealth Necessary to Meet Income Shortfall

Retirement Income Shortfall \$_____ (Step 5) × 20 = Wealth Necessary to Meet Income Shortfall

You're probably confused over why we multiplied your income shortfall by twenty. This is equivalent to assuming that you'll draw down your wealth at a rate of 5 percent a year. If you plan on taking 10 percent of your wealth as income then the number would be ten. If you plan on taking 20 percent of your wealth as income then the number would be 5. This number is derived by dividing your draw down rate into 100.

Step 9: Net Wealth Surplus/Shortage

Wealth Necessary to Meet Income Shortfall (Step 8) \$_____ + Required Inheritance Wealth (Step 6) − Future Value of Current Non-Employment Investments (Step 7) = Net Wealth Surplus/Shortage

If you have a surplus, then your current wealth covers your projected income shortfall. You're done with this work. If you have a wealth shortage, you must do two additional steps.

Step 10: Required Savings to Reach Wealth Shortfall

Net Wealth Shortfall \$_____ ÷ Annuity Discount Factor _____ = Required Additional Yearly Savings \$_____

Again, you need to know years to retirement and a rate of return you're earning on your retirement investments. Let's return to our illustration under step 7 and assume you're twenty years away from retirement and you'll earn 7 percent on your investments. Now go to appendix 2, column 7 percent and row 20. The number in the cell is 40.9955. If you divide your net wealth shortfall by this number it will tell you how much you must save each year to accumulate your net wealth shortfall.

Step 11: Required Additional Savings

Required Additional Yearly Savings \$_____ (Step 10) – Current Retirement Savings \$_____ = Surplus/Shortfall \$_____

If you have a surplus, that's great. You can continue with your current savings plan and give yourself a cushion of safety or you can spend more on consumption.

If you're short on savings then you must ask yourself whether you can afford to boost your savings rate. If you can't then you must extend your age of retirement or change your targeted income goal or change your inheritance goal or some combination of the three.

This is really what retirement planning is all about: making tradeoffs between competing ends.

THE COLLEGE PLANNING PROBLEM

When constructing a college savings plan, you need to consider your saving period, its future cost, your family's share of college cost, methods of saving for college, and types of assets suitable for college savings.

Saving Period

This is just the number of years before your children start college.

Future Cost Question

Everyone is concerned about college costs. For 2012–2013, the College Board has reported in-state public college costs averaging $22,261 and private college cost averaging $43,289 per year.

Five categories makeup these costs: tuition, fees, housing and meals, books and supplies, and personal and transportation costs.

Tuition is what colleges charge for instruction. Two things to be aware of with tuition fees is the difference between in state and out-of-state tuition and some schools charge different tuition rates for different majors.

Parents and students are often surprised by school fees. Fees cover the gamut from ID cards, health insurance, athletic facility usage, laboratory supplies, graduation expenses, computer access, studio usage, bus service, and student activities. Don't ignore these costs. They can become significant. Make sure you inquire at any college you plan on attending what student fees average a year.

Room and board is self-explanatory. Schools typically offer multiple housing and meal options. Sometimes living off campus can actually be the cheapest decision. Schools also differ in their residential policies. Some schools insist that freshmen live on campus. Avoiding these costs is one of the largest benefits of attending a local college and living at home. The College Board reports that average room and board costs in 2012–2013 went from $9,205 at four-year public college to $10,462 at private schools.

Many colleges publish the average costs for books and supplies at their institution. The College Board estimates these costs to be between $1,000 and $1,500 per year. There are strategies for minimizing book costs: buy used textbooks, buy previous editions of a required book (often they cover almost exactly the same material), buy books online instead of using the campus bookstore, rent books, see if the school library has the textbook and take it out for free, and share books. Also, many professors provide as handouts all the material you'll really ever need to pass the course. Consider not buying a textbook.

Finally, there are personal costs and transportation. Don't kid yourself, these costs add up to be significant. The College Board reports these expenses to run from $2,500 to over $3,000 for 2012–2013.

One reason we date our cost numbers is because in the future we know they will be greater. Over the past ten years tuition at private colleges have risen 60 percent while at public colleges 104 percent. When projecting future college costs you must build into your calculation expected price increases. We recommend assuming at least a 5 percent, per year, rise in college costs.

Let's work an example to show you what we mean. Your daughter is ten years away from attending college. You plan on her going to a state university that now costs in total $20,000 per year. Assuming a 5 percent rise in costs per year, you must plan your family's cost to be $32,578 a year.

To make this calculation, go to appendix 1, column 5 percent and row 10. The number in the cell is 1.6289. When you multiply $20,000 by this cell number you arrive at its future value of $32,578.

All of this can be quite discouraging. This is one reason more and more students are attending community colleges were costs are more manageable. One strategy is to attend a community college for your first two years of education and then transfer to a four-year college for your last two years. A second strategy to deal with these costs is to bargain. Parents and students often don't realize that a college's sticker price is meaningless. Don't be afraid to shop for the best deal you can find.

Deciding Your Share of College Costs

Colleges use formulas to allocate their cost among parents, students, and themselves. Colleges begin with their sticker price, subtract what they want parents to contribute, determine what they want the student to contribute and then make up any shortfall with grants, scholarships, et cetera.

There's a federal government methodology for calculating a family's share of these costs depending on your income and wealth that the College Scholarship Service of the College Board publishes.

Visit the College Board's website at www.collegeboard.org. They have a calculator designed to estimate college costs.

Paying College Costs

The least expensive way of paying college costs is out of savings and investments. This means beginning a college savings program the day your child is born. Paying for college out of current income reduces your standard of living. Paying for college with loans has become common.

To most parents, we recommend that their children help pay for college by taking out student loans as opposed to the parents taking a second mortgage on their home. Students can obtain low interest loans that they pay back over a working life of rising incomes. When children attend college, many parents are in the part of their life cycle when they should be acquiring assets and not liabilities. All colleges offer students opportunities to earn work-study money.

STUDENT AID AND FISCAL
RESPONSIBILITY ACT (PASSED 2010)

Starting in 2014, private banks will no longer be able to mediate federal student loans. All federal loans will be given through the Department of Education's federal Direct Loan Program. This will save students money on loan transaction costs. Second, all graduated students will be required to pay only 10 percent of their income in loan repayment. Third, students who select careers in public service (e.g., teaching, military, nursing) will see their loans forgiven after ten years of on-time payments. The act also reduced the forgiveness period for all other student loans to twenty years. Finally, the act increases Pell Grant money to students with financial—remember, Pell Grant money does not have to be repaid.

Saving for College

The easiest way to save for college is to take advantage of one or more of the college savings programs. If you begin to save when your child is born, it's relatively pretty easy to build up a large college fund for each of your children. This is the cheapest way of paying for college because you can take advantage of compound interest. Like the pursuit of all goals that require saving and investing, the sooner you start, the easier it becomes.

Five basic savings programs exist for college savings: uniform gift to minor account (UGMA), prepaid tuition plans, educational Coverdell IRAs, taxable savings, and the 529 plan. Each of these has their strengths and weaknesses. In the next chapter we cover the Coverdell. We ignore taxable savings programs.

UGMA is effectively a trust setup by parents for children that can contain cash, stocks, bonds, mutual funds, annuities, and life insurance policies. Donors to an UGMA irrevocably gift it. Assets in the trust belong to the minor but are controlled by the trust's custodian until the minor reaches the age of termination. Most UGMAs end at eighteen.

Reported income from a UGMA is on the child's tax return and thus taxed at the child's rate. Neither the donor nor the custodian can place any restrictions on the use of the money when the minor becomes an adult. Once a child reaches the age of termination all trust assets belong to them. They can use the money in the trust for any purpose. This means that a child doesn't have to use their UGMA assets for education. Most parents consider this a significant drawback. In addition, because UGMA accounts are in the name of a single child, assets in the trust are not transferrable to another beneficiary.

Another problem with UGMAs is that for financial aid purposes, colleges treat them as a student asset. This can have a large impact on financial aid eligibility.

On the upside, UGMAs give parents the freedom to contribute any amount of money they wish.

Prepaid tuition programs allow families to buy public in-state education at today's price. This acts as a hedge against inflation. Parents can either purchase a percentage of college tuition or credit hours.

Unfortunately, prepaid programs also have many downsides: participation is limited to state residents; they're mostly geared to in-state public institutions; they have high refund and cancellation costs; and prepaid programs often have a narrow definition of a college expense.

A very popular way of saving for college is a state sponsored 529 savings plan. Anyone can set-up a 529 and you can invest over $300,000 per beneficiary in many state plans. A 529 can even be created to help pay for graduate education.

There are many benefits to 529 plans. Although 529 contributions are after tax, contributions grow tax-deferred for federal reporting purposes, and distributions to pay for a beneficiary's college are also free of federal income taxes. State taxes vary on 529 contributions and distributions.

Parents control the assets in a 529 and not the named beneficiary. Parents can even reclaim 529 funds. The earnings portion of nonqualified withdrawals is subject to taxes and penalties. Furthermore, a 529 plan is easy to create and maintain. Once an enrollment form is completed, all you do is contribute to it. A professional manages plan assets. If you have more than one child any money the first child doesn't need can be passed to another sibling. Also, 529 money can be spent in any state, not just the state it was set up in.

The biggest drawback with 529 plans is that states dictate the allowable asset allocations for these plans. If your state's 529 offers age based asset allocations, consider selecting this option. This option allows a fund manager to shift investments from more aggressive to less aggressive as your child approaches college age. Before investing, be sure to check what choices your state plan offers.

Coverdell Educational Savings Accoun

A Coverdell Education Savings Account (ESA) helps parents and students save for education expenses. Maximum contribution per beneficiary cannot exceed $2,000 a year. To be a beneficiary, a person must be less than eighteen years of age.

Coverdell contributions are not tax deductible, however, investments grow tax free until distributed. If distributions are less than a beneficiary's qualified education expenses then no tax is owed. However, if distributions exceed qualified education expenses, a tax penalty is applied to this portion.

The Coverdell can be applied to schooling from elementary grades through higher education.

College Investment Strategies

After deciding on the best college savings program(s) for your family, your next step is figure out how to allocate your college savings between stocks, bonds, and cash equivalents. When you begin to save, the age of your children strongly influences this decision.

Children Zero to Twelve

Absolutely the best time to begin saving for your children's education is at birth. This gives you approximately eighteen years to stay invested. At least for the first twelve years, a portfolio weighed toward a mix of United States and international stock mutual funds can make good sense.

Children Twelve to Fourteen

If you began a savings plan when your child was born, then probably this is the time to begin moving some of your investments out of stocks and into intermediate-term bonds (i.e., bonds that mature within five to seven years) and cash assets. How much money should you move? Transfer enough money to cover their first year in college. Leave the rest in your stock portfolio.

If you're beginning a college savings plan, then you have missed investing in the stock market. Given the propensity of stock markets to turn down severely and their normal recovery period, good advice dictates not investing in stocks. Where should you invest? Bonds and cash assets are your best alternatives.

Children Fourteen to Eighteen

If you started an early savings plan, when your child is approximately fifteen years of age, remove their sophomore year money out of your stock portfolio; when they are sixteen, remove their junior year money; and finally, at seventeen, remove their senior year money.

This removed money needs to be invested in safer assets such as short or medium term bond funds and cash assets.

If you're just beginning a college savings plan, your only real option is bonds and cash assets. For most people, starting to save when a child is fourteen to eighteen means delayed retirement or forcing children to take on a greater part of the burden of attending college.

STARTING YOUR CHILDREN
ON THEIR LIFETIME SAVINGS PROGRAM

This is an exciting area of investing. One of the greatest gifts we can give any person is the freedom to choose the life they want. One way of giving this gift to your children is to begin them on a lifetime savings program at birth. For a relatively small amount of yearly savings, you can start each of your children on an easy to follow savings program, which if followed, accumulates to a million dollars by the time they reach their middle fifties.

Let's say that you want to start your children on a savings program that will culminate in them each having a $1,000,000 at age fifty-five. How much do you have to save each year from birth to achieve this goal? Assuming a 7 percent annual rate of return (generated by a well-diversified pure stock portfolio), the answer is $1,736 a year. For many Americans, this is affordable for parents to begin and affordable for children to continue. Like all savings goals, the longer you wait to begin, the more burdensome the savings requirement becomes. Wait just ten years to begin this program and the annual cost rises to $3,500. Wait fifteen years and the cost becomes $5,009 a year.

15

A Survey of
Retirement Savings Plans

SOME BASIC ADVICE

Save, save, and then save some more. No one knows what the future will bring. Other than poor financial planning, the greatest enemy of retirement savings is inflation. In this century, the long-term US inflation rate has been about 3 percent per year. At 3 percent, inflation will cut the purchasing power of your money by 50 percent in just twenty-five years. Therefore, it's important to invest your long-term savings in financial assets that offset inflation.

As stated in chapter 6, the one financial asset that can beat inflation in the long-run is stock. This suggests investing retirement savings in stock mutual funds, especially if you're ten or more years away from retirement.

Take advantage of every tax-deductible, tax-deferred, corporate, or individual retirement plan available to you. In many of these, employers also match what you contribute. This means that either Uncle Sam or your employer or both are subsidizing your retirement. All of the tax deferrals that exist in retirement plans are capable of rapid wealth accumulation. In addition, many retirement plans allow you opportunities to tap into them for college loans.

Finally, own your own home. As stated earlier, why throw rent money away? Also, homes are a great inflation hedge. Our only caveat when it comes to purchasing a house is not to over-invest in it. Aside from periods of inflation, home appreciation is often less than stock returns.

EMPLOYER PENSION PLANS

Defined-Benefit Plan

These plans are becoming extinct. Companies are terminating them. If you're in a defined-benefit plan, check if it has an automatic cost of living adjustment (COLA). Many don't. Without a COLA, you're not protected from inflation. In addition, you're entitled to an individual benefit statement once a year. Start requesting it so that you can track the size of your pension credit.

Job-hopping reduces the size of the benefit you receive from this type of plan. Defined-benefit plans provide the largest payouts to those who stay at the same place of employment the longest.

Find out the extent to which your company integrates its pension with Social Security. Under integration, your Social Security benefit partly reduces pension benefits.

If you earn an average salary, don't worry about this type of pension plan going bankrupt. The Pension Benefit Guaranty Corporation insures defined-benefit plans up to a certain limit.

Defined-Contribution

This type of plan has gained great popularity. In a defined-contribution plan, employees contribute to their own retirement and select their investments. Employers often match up to a certain percentage what employees contribute.

The better-known defined-contribution plans are the 401(k) and 403(b), stock-bonus plans, employee stock ownership plans, employee Keogh plans, and SIMPLE employee pensions.

The amount of money you receive at retirement from a defined contribution plan depends on how much you invest and how well your investments perform. In this type of plan, no guarantees are given.

Traditional 401(k)

How does a 401(k) work? You tell your employer to set aside a certain percentage of your income to invest in the company's plan. You don't pay federal income tax on this money and the accumulations are tax-free until you withdraw it. The government subsidizes your savings. The contribution limit for 2013 is $17,500 per year for those under fifty and $23,000 for those over fifty. These caps adjust upward with inflation over time.

Most employers match up to a certain percentage of your contributions. The tax portion of this money is free. The minimum contribution you should make is at least what your company will match.

What kinds of investments can you make in a 401(k) plan? Most companies offer their employees a variety of investment choices. These include money market funds, bond funds, stock funds, and even investing in the company's stock.

You shouldn't invest more than 15 percent of your portfolio in your company's stock. Many apparently good companies go bankrupt and if all your retirement is invested in your company's stock, you may find yourself without any retirement wealth. One company we worked with went bankrupt and its share price went from $130 to $1 in one year. Many of its employees went from a net worth of over 1 million dollars to $30,000. This is what happens when your retirement savings lacks diversification. Avoid this situation and split your investment dollars into a variety of different investments.

Roth 401(k)

This works like a traditional 401(k) except it's funded with after tax dollars. There is no current tax benefit but it grows tax deferred and when you take your money out it is tax-free income except for employer's match. The contribution limitations are the same as a traditional 401(k).

Whether a 401(k) or Roth 401(k) is best for you depends on your age and future earnings potential.

If you're young (middle twenties) then a Roth 401(k) might make a lot of sense since the taxes you pay on your contributions now will probably be less than the taxes you pay on your withdrawals under a traditional 401(k) when you're in a higher tax bracket.

If you can't afford the tax bill on your Roth 401(k) then consider dividing your annual contributions between a traditional 401(k) and a Roth 401(k).

In deciding between a traditional 401(k) and a Roth 401(k) we advise that you speak with a financial counselor.

403(b)

This is the tax-deferred plan for those who make their living as part of an educational, charitable, or religious organization. 403(b)s work like 401(k)s.

Money invested in a 403(b) is pretax income and it grows tax-deferred. Your maximum contribution rules are the same as 401(k)s. Employer matches aren't as common in this type of plan as they are in a 401(k). Roth 403(b)s may also be available.

SIMPLE and SEP IRAs

SIMPLE stands for savings incentive match plan for employees. SIMPLEs are only available to firms with fewer than one hundred employees who don't currently offer any other retirement plan. A SIMPLE is easier to administer than a 401(k).

As of 2013, SIMPLEs allow for employee contributions up to $12,000 or 100 percent of compensation if less than $12,000 with a catch-up limit of $2,500 for employees fifty or older. If you participate in a SIMPLE IRA, your employer could match the contributions you make to the plan, up to 3 percent of your salary. Even if you don't make contributions, your employer must make a flat contribution on your behalf of 2 percent of your salary. All contributions are immediately vested.

A SEP is for any self-employed individual, business owner, or individual who earns more than $550 in self-employment income a year. SEPs are easy to set up and maintain. SEPs only allow for employer contributions. For 2013, the maximum annual contribution is the lesser of $51,000 or 25 percent of annual compensation (i.e., self-employed income).

A SEP has no catch-up provision. Contributions are immediately vested and employees under twenty-one may be excluded.

For both SEP and SIMPLE IRAs Roth accounts are not allowed, pre-tax money goes in and is taxed as ordinary income when taken out at retirement (no earlier than fifty-nine-and-a-half). If money is removed before the age of fifty-nine-and-a-half there is a 10 percent penalty on top of income taxes.

Keogh Plan

Keogh plans can be set up as either a defined benefit plan (structured like a traditional pension plan) or a defined contribution plan (structured more like a 401(k)).

As a defined-contribution plan, you can contribute up to 25 percent of your earned income. Defined-contribution Keogh can be structured either as a profit-sharing plan or a money-purchase plan. As a profit sharing plan you have more flexibility in making contributions. A money-purchase Keogh forces you into a fixed contribution scale.

Keoghs set up as a defined-benefit plan guarantees plan participants a set annual payment. Contributions must be calibrated to ensure that the plan will be able to provide this payment even in unprofitable years. You'll need an actuary to handle these calculations.

Under Keogh plans, you must offer your employees the same options you provide yourself. Therefore, it's important to check with your accountant before embarking on it or any company-wide retirement program.

Like all other retirement tax shelters you must wait until you are fifty-nine-and-a-half before taking contributions out without facing a slew of penalties. However, if you terminate your business and you're at least fifty-five you can begin receiving plan distributions without penalty.

Section 457 Plans

This plan is available to state and local government employees. Loans aren't allowed against this money and employer contributions are rarely made. The employer manages the funds in this plan.

IRA Personal Savings Plans

When it comes to retirement, IRA (Individual Retirement Account) has become the most important three letters in the American lexicon. IRAs complement pension plan savings. Three types of IRAs are traditional, Roth, and college.

INDIVIDUAL RETIREMENT ACCOUNTS

Traditional IRA

What is a traditional IRA? It's an account you set up with a bank, a brokerage house, a mutual fund company, and others where you invest your money in stocks, bonds, and cash assets. This account is self-directed—which means that you have to make all investment choices.

For 2013 maximum contributions are $5,500 if you're forty-nine or younger and $6,500 if you're fifty and older. All contributions must come out of earned income and your earned income must equal or exceed total yearly contributions.

If you have sufficient earned income, you may make an IRA contribution for a nonworking spouse in addition to your own IRA contribution.

If you participate in a work related retirement plan then you can't make a deduction for a contribution to your traditional IRA. However, you can still make nondeductible IRA contributions and your investments will grow tax deferred until your time of withdrawal.

120 Chapter 15

Roth IRA

A Roth IRA allows a maximum contribution equal to a traditional IRA. The difference between Roth and a traditional IRA is that Roth allows no current year tax break on money you invest. So why bother with a Roth IRA?

- At any time, you can withdraw money from your Roth IRA and not pay taxes on money you contributed. This isn't true for a traditional IRA.
- After a Roth is five years old, you can remove your profits tax-free once you reach the age of fifty-nine-and-a-half. This isn't true for a traditional IRA.
- You can contribute to a Roth forever. This isn't true for a traditional IRA. In a traditional IRA, once you reach age seventy-and-a-half, you have to start withdrawing money from it—which means that you must start paying taxes.
- You can leave your Roth to heirs and they can contribute to it forever. Remember, though, that their contributions, like yours, must come from after-tax dollars.

Children can also use the Roth to start a savings program and even save for college. The kicker is that the child must earn income. Children may contribute up to their earned income or current limit per year—whichever is less. In 2013 this limit was $5,500.

If you child earns $2,000, they can invest this money in a Roth and you can reimburse them through a $2,000 gift. Of course, they'll have to file a tax return. One advantage of your child starting a college savings program with Roth is that under Roth rules, the money they contributed isn't taxed again and they pay no penalty on early withdrawal. They will have to pay taxes on the dividends and capital appreciation portion of the amount withdrawn.

Annuities

Annuities are an insurance product that allows someone to pay a single amount or a series of payment to the insurance company with a promise of future lifetime payments back to you. The purpose is to provide a steady stream of income. The income normally would be for retirement purposes.

There are three ways that payments are structured when you begin to annuitize an annuity. Annuitizing just means we are beginning to receive monthly payments from the insurance company. First method is single life, which typically means the payment is calculated on the life expectancy of the owner of the policy. The older the person the higher the monthly payments will be due to the expected shorter time they will have to make those payments. The second method is both husband and wife's life. What that means is payments will continue until both individuals have died. Because it is covering both wife and husband the monthly payments will be less than just a single life. The third most common method is term certain. Under term certain monthly payments will be paid for a specific number of years, no matter how long the owner lives.

Terminology

- Single premium the policy fully pays for the annuity with a single payment.
- Flexible premium annuities are funded with series of payments.
- Deferred annuity means you pay for the annuity now and start monthly payments sometime in the future.
- Immediate annuities are funded with a single payment and monthly income starts immediately.
- Fixed annuity typically guarantees some minimum return and is not exposed to the risk of the market.
- Variable annuities allows the policy owner to select from a variety of investment for the money to go into, but this does put the money at the risk of the market.

Annuities can be a good product for individuals who have a very low tolerance for risk and looking for a fixed income for the rest of their life.

16

Action Plan

You're now ready to build a financial plan. The only way to become financially successful is to act on your knowledge. It's up to you to take charge of your future. It takes a conscious effort to begin and maintain a financial plan. Our experience is that without a plan, most people backslide quickly into destructive spending habits. It's our objective not only to educate you, but also to help motivate you to begin the process of making yourself financially healthy.

At this point, you should have completed the following steps:

Step 1: Stated your financial goals and divided them into short-, medium-, and long-terms. To each goal, you assigned a current dollar amount.

Step 2: Adjusted your financial goals for inflation. Don't ignore this step. Inflation is a permanent part of the US economy. The corrosive power of inflation on wealth is substantial even when its levels seem nonthreatening. A mere 3 percent inflation rate means that over fifty years, the purchasing power of a dollar declines to $0.25.

Step 3: Calculated the savings cost for each of your goals. This is a critical step in constructing an *Action Plan*. You also calculated the cost of paying off all of your credit card debt.

Step 4: Tracked your spending for a month or longer. Entered in your tracking sheets is this information. Learning how money is spent is a necessary part of gaining control over your finances.

Step 5: Analyzed your insurance needs. Before starting an investment program you should review your life, disability, medical, and home

insurance needs. Even if you're a college student, don't ignore this
step.

Step 6: Reviewed a summary of your Social Security benefits statement.
Knowing what to expect from Social Security at retirement is a necessary step in retirement planning—especially if you're fifty or older.

You're now ready to build your *Action Plan*.

DEVELOP AN ACTION PLAN

By now, you know a lot about your personal finances. This last step deals
with the most difficult aspect of personal savings and investing: building
a financial plan into your budget. What we want to do in this last step is
demonstrate how to build a savings and investment program into your
budget.

Calculating Your Savings Shortfall

First, calculate your monthly disposable income. This is the actual money
you have to spend from your income each month. It equals your gross
monthly income minus all deductions made from your pay. (Get this
information from your pay stub.)

1. Net take home pay   _____
2. Subtract amount needed for goals   -_____
3. Subtract monthly fixed expenses   -_____
4. Subtract monthly variable expenses   -_____
5. Total surplus/(shortage)   _____

If you have a surplus even after funding all your goals, then you can
move forward. If you are short income and step 5 is a negative number,
you should review your variable expenses for areas where you may want
to reduce the amount spent each month. A second option would be to
modify your goals. What we mean by this is taking a goal and reducing the amount you are trying to achieve which would in turn lower the
amount needed to reach the goal. Another option is to remove the goal for
now and when your income goes up, put the goal back into the plan. If
you chose to reduce the amount of the goal(s) and your income improves,
take a portion of your pay increase and apply some of the raise toward
your goals that were previously reduced.

If you take half of each annual raise or promotion and apply it toward
your goals, two things will happen: first, you will still have more take

home pay each month; and second, you will be increasing dollars going toward goals, which turns into wealth. So if you are a little short on the amount needed to fund your retirement, just increase the amount each year when you get a raise. Before you know it, the amount going into retirement or some other goal will be more than you ever thought you could afford. Best of all—you will never miss the money if you start it the same week your pay increase goes into effect. Painless and easy!!!

How to Remove Financial Roadblocks

Reduce Your Variable Expenses

If you can't reach your financial goals, the first thing to do is to eliminate unnecessary variable costs from your budget. Obvious places to look for savings are to cut back on your cell phone and cable TV services. Most people also have overblown food and entertainment expenses. Learn to shop more wisely and take advantage of coupons and other freebies. Eat out less and stop buying expensive bottles of water and cups of coffee. Believe us, if you look carefully you'll find many variable expenses to eliminate or cut back.

Reduce Your Fixed Costs

Almost everyone also has overblown fixed costs. Switch to less expensive loans and credit cards. Save on your utility bills by shutting off lights and not letting water run. Eliminate unnecessary insurance. Look for cheaper insurance rates. Take larger deductibles on your insurance policies and cut your monthly insurance bills.

Bolster Your Income

That's right, we're telling you to work more or look for a higher paying job (most people undersell themselves in labor markets). Go for a promotion. Retrain yourself to get a higher paying job. (Currently, the unemployment rate is high and our advice might sound crazy. However, eventually jobs will return.)

Lengthen the Time to Reach Your Financial Goals

By extending the time you want to reach a financial goal, you lower its monthly cost. Recalculate the monthly cost of your different savings goals, like retirement, by plugging in different time scenarios. Adding a few years to your retirement goal can have a large effect on its monthly cost.

Eliminate Some of Your Financial Goals

Try eliminating some of your financial goals. Don't eliminate goals like paying off your credit card debt or funding retirement. Drop other goals like a vacation home or boat. Even consider cutting back on how much you contribute to your children's education. Instead of planning to send your children to a private university, consider a public university. Let your children borrow more money for college—they're young and have a lifetime to pay back their loans.

Invest More Aggressively

Each of us has a comfortable level of risk we're willing to tolerate. One way of making financial goals more affordable is to increase your risk exposure. More risks means higher returns and a lower cost of funding a financial goal. We're not talking about gambling. However, by choosing a portfolio more heavily weighted with stock, you'll increase its return and also increase your exposure to risk.

Engage in Life Cycle Saving and Investing

Life cycle saving and investing recognizes that at different stages of your life you can afford to save different amounts of money. When you're young, your income is going to be lower, and thus you should save less. As you age, your income rises and you can afford to save more. Of course, as you become older your living expenses also rise.

Life cycle saving and investing requires special software that matches your lifetime earnings with a savings and investment program. Many financial planners use this tool. Definitely look into this option when planning your financial future.

17

✛

College Choices
and Student Loans

When you are around eighteen you face two choices that will affect the rest of your life.

Choice 1: After graduating high school, should I keep going to school or should I enter the workplace?

Choice 2: Whatever post-secondary (after high school) school I attend, what skill should I learn or what major should I select?

Both of these choices will influence whether you're employed or unemployed and how much money you will earn. These choices will also determine the level of your future life satisfaction—probably, the most important of all considerations.

SHOULD I KEEP ON TRUCKIN'?

The answer is yes. The evidence is clear: more training and more education after high school means a lower chance of becoming unemployed and higher future earnings.

If you complete a four year college degree there is around a 60 percent wage premium over having just a high school degree. This means that for every $1 you would have earned as a high school graduate, you'll now earn around $1.60. This wage premium collapses to just about 15 percent to 20 percent if you attend college but never finish. It's a fool's errand to start college and never finish. The money is in getting your college degree.

In fact, going even past the college degree to a graduate degree (masters or doctorate) adds an additional wage premium of around 30 percent.

Going forward in time, here's what the 2020 projected job outlook looks like:

- Through 2020 there will be 55 million job openings.
- Thirty-five percent of these job opportunities require at least a bachelor's degree. Thirty percent will require some college or a community college degree. The rest will require just a high school degree.
- The fastest growing job opportunities are going to be in STEM (science, technology, engineering and mathematics), healthcare professions, healthcare support, and community services.
- Employers want from employees good cognitive skills such as communication and analytics.
- Given current projections, there will be a shortfall of 5 million workers with the necessary post-secondary education.

WHAT MAJOR SHOULD I CHOOSE?

Not all college majors are created equal. Current unemployment rates among recent college graduates run from around 5 percent to 15 percent—a significant difference. The overall unemployment rate for recent graduates is about 8 percent. For those with advanced degrees it drops to approximately 3 percent.

Recent undergraduate majors with the lowest unemployment rates include nursing, elementary education, physical fitness, parks and recreation, chemistry, and finance.

Recent undergraduate majors with the highest unemployment rates include political science, film-video-photography arts, anthropology, architecture, and information systems (clerical function).

Fields of study where recent graduates have had the toughest time gaining traction in the labor market include: social sciences, arts, and humanities. Unemployment rates among all three areas hover around 10 percent. One bright spot was among foreign language majors who had an average unemployment rate of about 8 percent.

10 Worst College Majors[1]

1. Family Consumer Sciences
   - Starting salary, $44,700 (median)
   - Mid-career salary, $47,800 (median)
   - Mid-career unemployment rate, 4.7 percent

2. Humanities
   - Starting salary, $35,600
   - Mid-career salary, $60,100
   - Mid-career unemployment rate, 9.8 percent
3. Mass Media
   - Starting salary, $34,400
   - Mid-career salary, $59,800
   - Mid-career unemployment rate, 7. percent
4. Studio Arts
   - Starting salary, $35,700
   - Mid-career salary, $53,200
   - Mid-career unemployment rate, 7.3 percent
5. Interdisciplinary Studies
   - Starting salary, $37,500
   - Mid-career salary, $51,000
   - Mid-career unemployment rate, 8.5 percent
6. Art History
   - Starting salary, $36,400
   - Mid-career salary, $54,000
   - Mid-career unemployment rate, 8.3 percent
7. Early Childhood Education
   - Starting salary, $29,200
   - Mid-career salary, $37,600
   - Mid-career unemployment rate, 5.5 percent
8. Social Work
   - Starting salary, $33,100
   - Mid-career salary, $45,300
   - Mid-career unemployment rate, 6.5 percent
9. Fine Arts
   - Starting salary, $31,800
   - Mid-career salary, $53,700
   - Mid-career unemployment rate, 7.3 percent
10. Human Services and Community Organization
    - Starting salary, $32,900
    - Mid-career salary, $53,700
    - Mid-career unemployment rate, 8.1 percent

10 Best Majors[2]

1. Pharmacy and Pharmaceutical Sciences
   - Starting salary, $42,100
   - Mid-career salary, $120,000
   - Mid-career unemployment rate, 2.5 percent

2. Computer Science
   - Starting salary, $58,400
   - Mid-career salary, $100,000
   - Mid-career unemployment rate, 4.7 percent
3. Civil Engineering
   - Starting salary, $53,800
   - Mid-career salary, $88,800
   - Mid-career unemployment rate, 4 percent
4. Information Systems Management
   - Starting salary, $51,600
   - Mid-career salary, $88,600
   - Mid-career unemployment rate, 4 percent
5. Nursing
   - Starting salary, $54,100
   - Mid-career salary, $70,200
   - Mid-career unemployment rate, 2.3 percent
6. Information Systems
   - Starting salary, $50,900
   - Mid-career salary, $86,700
   - Mid-career unemployment rate, 4.4 percent
7. Finance
   - Starting salary, $47,700
   - Mid-career salary, $85,400
   - Mid-career unemployment rate, 4.4 percent
8. Math
   - Starting salary, $48,500
   - Mid-career salary, $85,800
   - Mid-career unemployment rate, 4.6 percent
9. Information Science
   - Starting salary, $54,100
   - Mid-career salary, $83,800
   - Mid-career unemployment rate, 5.2 percent
10. Construction (Management)
    - Starting salary, $49,500
    - Mid-career salary, $86,100
    - Mid-career unemployment rate, 4.7 percent

Table 17.1. Top Paid Majors Upon Graduation[3]

Major	Average Starting Salary
Petroleum Engineering	$96,200
Computer Engineering	$70,300
Chemical Engineering	$66,900
Computer Science	$64,100
Aerospace/Aeronautical/Astronautical Engineering	$63,900
Mechanical Engineering	$63,900
Electrical/Electronics and Communications Engineering	$62,500
Engineering Technology	$60,900
Management Information Systems/Business	$60,300
Logistics/Materials Management	$59,500

FEDERAL LOAN OPTIONS[4] AND REPAYMENT PLANS

These plans apply to Federal Direct Loans, Federal Family Education Loans, Parent PLUS, and Stafford Loans.

- *Standard Repayment*: This is the starting plan. Payments are normally at least $50 a month and target your repayment time to ten years.
- *Graduated Repayment Plan*: Assumes you begin with a lower paying career after college and your income will increase over time. Loan payments begin low and increase over time. Target repayment to be ten years.
- *Extended Repayment Plan*: Assumes you can't afford standard or graduated repayments. Extend loans out twenty-five years with either fixed or graduated payments.
- *Income-Based, Pay as you Earn, Income Contingent and Income Sensitive Plans*: Makes student loan repayments based on what you can afford.
- *Deferment and Forbearance*: Allows you to temporarily suspend loan payments.

Before selecting any of these options do the following three things:

1. Get organized. Go to www.nsids.ed.gov to view all of your federal student loans.
2. Go to the Federal Student Aid Repayment Estimator at studentloans. gov/myDirectLoan/repaymentEstimatorLoginRedirect.action and figure out your repayment options
3. Contact your loan servicer. Your loan servicer can help you select the best repayment plan. To find out whose servicing your federal loans go to www.nsids.ed.gov.

Important Facts to Know About Federal Student Loans

- You can prepay student loans. Make sure any extra money you want to pay is applied against your principal balance. Always make these extra payments toward your loans with the highest interest rates.
- If you're having problems making loan payments don't stick your head in the sand. Immediately contact your loan servicer and work out a solution.
- You can't default (not pay) your student loans. Missed payments are reported to the credit bureaus. This will affect your FICO score. In addition, if you stop making payments legal action will be taken against you including garnishment of wages and withholding of tax refunds.
- Within 120 days of receiving a loan you can cancel it by returning all money without interest or fees charged.
- If you enter certain occupations—public service, AmeriCorps, PeaceCorps, teaching, nursing—some part of your student loans will be forgiven. Go to IBRinfo.org to find out more.
- Debt consolidation is an option you should investigate. Speak to an expert if this option makes sense for you.

NOTES

1. From Kiplinger, September, 2013, www.kiplinger.com/slideshow/college/T012-S001-worst-college-majors-for-your-career/.

2. From Kiplinger, September, 2013, www.kiplinger.com/slideshow/business/T012-S001-10-best-college-majors-for-a-lucrative-career/index.html.

3. From Kiplinger, September, 2013, www.kiplinger.com/slideshow/business/T012-S001-10-best-college-majors-for-a-lucrative-career/index.html.

4. Go to appendix 3 for a current list of federal loan options. We don't discuss these in the body of the text.

18

Reasons People Fail
in the World of Investments

Procrastination

Many of us look at retirement and college planning as something we'll begin tomorrow. Avoid this type of reasoning. The longer you wait to begin saving and investing, the greater your savings burden to reach your goals. The shorter time you have to accumulate money for your goals the more you'll have to select an aggressive investment strategy that increases your risk exposure.

Lack of Specific Goals

Most people have poorly defined financial goals such as "I want to retire someday," "I want to send my kids to a good college," "I want to take care of my parents when they get older," et cetera. Goals like these are difficult to achieve. Financial goals, to become an active force in your life (and even exert pressure on you to accomplish), must be clearly and fully stated in terms of a definite sum of money and time period. "In twenty years, I want to retire on an income of $65,000 per year." "In ten years, I want $100,000 for my child's college education." Goals have a greater chance of success when properly stated.

Living Beyond Your Means

Look at our friend. She's anxious and in a sweat because she can't pay her bills. She spends more money than she earns. If you want to reach financial goals, you must learn to spend less than you earn. The real secret to achieving this is to first pay for your financial goals. If you're not willing to take care of your future, who will? Once your future is financed, you can spend the rest of your money on the here and now.

Fear of the Unknown

One reason many people invest in savings accounts and CDs, instead of stock and bond mutual funds, is fear of the unknown. Making you comfortable with the jargon and logic of personal investing is a prime goal of our book. Investing isn't as hard as it appears. With a little homework and careful planning, most of you can manage your own portfolio.

Buying When Prices are Too High

Ideally, if you're a market day trader—these are people who try to outfox financial markets in the short-term—you buy financial assets when their prices are low and sell them when prices are high. (As an aside, day trading is much too risky and we don't recommend it.) What does the average investor do? They'll wait on the sideline until a market boom has matured (which means that stock prices are too high and likely will go down), then they buy into the market, asset prices soon drop, then they panic and sell. They buy high and sell low. This makes no sense. Dollar cost averaging overcomes this problem by limiting your purchase of financial assets when prices are high and buying more financial assets when prices are low. This is the way you're supposed to invest.

Miscalculating Time and Money

Miscalculating time is a type of procrastination. Most of you neglect to consider how fast a lifetime of days, weeks, and years pass. Get rid of the thought that tomorrow will be the time to start. "Tomorrows" come and go fast. Before we know it, twenty years have passed and you're behind in your retirement and college savings plans. Now is time to start your savings and investment program!

Falling in Love with an Investment

You're not required to marry your investments for life—save that type of love for a spouse. How often have you had an old pair of shoes, a comfortable shirt or a perfect fitting pair of jeans that you didn't want to throw out? You can develop that same kind of feeling toward a financial investment. Don't do it. Unless an investment is performing to your expectations, get rid of it.

Ignoring Investment Opportunities

At this point, your head is probably spinning with investment options. Many people we advise ignore investment opportunities out of either ignorance or fear. A primary concern for many of us is to keep invested money safe. This isn't the way to build long-term financial security. Some managed risk exposure is necessary to achieve substantial financial goals.

Losing Patience

Don't follow your investments moment by moment. Prices of financial assets move up and down daily. Seeing a pattern in your investment portfolio requires viewing it from a multiple year perspective. Mutual fund stock investing requires you stay invested at least seven to ten years. Unfortunately, many of us are too quick to panic when we experience a financial downturn. The natural tendency is to pull investments that don't perform well in the short-run and reinvest them in safe assets such as saving accounts or CDs. Avoid this type of behavior. Each class of asset has a recognized investment horizon that's appropriate for its historical performance. You need to understand these before investing.

Following a Tip

Most hot tips fail to turn into great investments. Free information is usually either wrong or dated. Dated means the "hot tip" is already in the prices of financial assets. This implies it's too late to make money by following it.

Ignorance about Taxes

One of your goals should be to avoid paying taxes on your investment gains. Many tax-deductible and tax-deferred investment vehicles exist—

discussed in the last chapter—to shelter your investments. Take advantage of them. Every dollar paid in taxes makes you poorer.

Almost as important as learning how to avoid taxes is calculating your tax bracket. We have ignored taxes in previous calculations. Without knowing your tax bracket, it's impossible to calculate exactly how much to save to reach any financial goal. Other issues, such as choosing between a traditional IRA and Roth, when you should begin withdrawing money from a traditional IRA, when it's worthwhile to invest in municipal bonds, all depend on knowing your tax bracket.

Buying Too Much Insurance

Don't overbuy insurance. Insurance is safety net, not an investment. For life insurance, insurance companies recommend eight to ten times your annual salary. We find this type of advice too simplistic. How much life insurance you should own, like all insurance needs, depends on a person's situation. If you're fifty-years of age, earn $55,000 a year, have almost no debt, rent an apartment, and have no family obligations, then why should you own life insurance? You probably shouldn't. Now assume this same individual is married, has a couple of kids, and is paying off a $150,000 mortgage. This person might want more than eight times their salary in life insurance.

Lack of Diversification

We've already discussed diversification. The benefit of diversification is that it reduces risk. In personal investing, it's never a question of whether or not you should diversify; it's always what form it should take.

Lack of Discipline to Follow Investment Tactics

Developing and maintaining a long-term financial plan is important to your future success and security. The difficulty is doing it and sticking with it. Our materials will help you with this problem. If you have come this far in your reading, assuming you have completed all of your steps, then you have done it! This is great. Most people never reach this point. Now you have to stick with it. The more you can take advantage of forced savings plans, the easier it is to invest. Defined-contribution plans have this feature. Most mutual fund companies also have automatic account builder programs. With your permission, they'll take money from your savings or checking account every month: no need to write a check or call to make an investment. This effectively creates a forced savings plan.

Ultimately, what you have to do is select a strategy and stick with it. This means not changing your mind every day. Once your plan is in place, the only thing that should cause you to alter it is if one of your key assumptions changes.

19

✛

How to Purchase Financial Assets

Many investors use a broker for their investing. This includes the purchasing and selling of stocks, bonds, cash assets, and mutual funds. Other alternatives exist. The cheapest way to buy a mutual fund is to buy it directly from the company issuing the fund via mail or electronic transfer (this is moving your money directly from your local bank electronically to a mutual fund company). Once you establish electronic transfer with a mutual fund company, you can invest automatically without any action on your part by giving the mutual fund company permission to take money from your checking account on a regular basis. This is a form of dollar cost averaging.

Most stocks trade through a broker. Broker's services range from full-service to discount service. A full-service broker will not only buy stocks for you but will also advise you on which stocks to purchase. Discount brokers don't offer advice. They just execute your purchase orders. The attractiveness of discount brokers is their reduced cost. Most full-service brokers will charge a flat rate, and a charge per stock share purchased.

Discount brokerage fees differ between companies, but most will offer a flat rate up to a certain number of shares traded or dollar amounts traded.

Online trading offers convenience and rock bottom costs per trade. This method of buying and selling is for the person who knows what they want. Some online trading companies experience processing problems. This is why you place limit prices on your trades. Limit prices specify maximum and minimum prices on your buy and sell stock orders. When selecting an online broker, look for one that can process trades quickly. Some online brokers offer a guarantee on their process time.

Some stocks are available directly from its issuing company. Companies that sell stock directly to investors often allow an automatic reinvestment of dividends as share purchasers. This program is called a dividend reinvestment program (DRIP). DRIPs are a great way for investors to start a dollar cost averaging program with little initial money.

Banks now offer investment services. Banks have always offered IRA CDs. Banks also now offer mutual funds. They act as an intermediary for the mutual fund company.

20

Information Sources
about Personal Finance

Information sources related to personal investing are endless. Finding information isn't a problem. What the new investor often finds difficult is locating specific information.

The first step in finding investment information is to decide what you want. Are you trying to determine the mix of financial assets appropriate for your age and goals? Are you trying to find the past performance record of a particular mutual fund? Are you trying to make a future value calculation? The correct information source depends on the type of question you ask.

Information Sources

Once you know what type of information you want, you can begin mining for it in various media outlets. Today's investor has seven main sources of information related to personal investing: regular and cable TV, newspapers, Internet, newsletters, investment clubs, radio, and magazines.

Television

We think the best TV sources for investment information are CNBC and Fox Business News. Both begin in the morning and end early evening. These daily show review every aspect of financial news and personal investing. Other excellent financial news programs exist on Bloomberg TV and CNN.

Internet

Three categories of websites you should investigate are broker, mutual fund, and financial planning sites. Broker sites are mostly for investors who invest in individual stocks. These broker sites offer online trading. A well-run broker site will offer you timely company research, portfolio tracking, twenty-four hour a day account access, and low trading costs.

Mutual fund companies, like Fidelity, sponsor mutual fund sites that analyze, screen, and track mutual funds. One site we like is Morningstar. com. At last count, this site was tracking ten thousand mutual funds. Morningstar also offers you free programs for portfolio tracking. Many services provided by Morningstar are without charge.

One boom area in financial Internet services has been in financial planning sites. These sites range from free to small yearly fees. Be careful when using a financial planning site. Remember you're dealing with a software program and not a person. While software programs have become more sophisticated, they still lack the complexity to deal with many individual problems. Nevertheless, we like many of these financial planning sites if they're not used mechanically. Given the changing nature and quality of these sites, we're not making any recommendation.

Newspapers

The premier newspapers for investing are the *Wall Street Journal* and *Investor's Daily*. Both discuss current financial news and provide financial tables listing individual investments including stocks, bonds, cash assets, mutual funds, options, futures, et cetera. In addition, you'll find articles on investment strategies, sector analysis, and detailed economic and political news stories.

Magazines

Kiplinger, *Mutual Funds*, and *Money Magazine* are great examples of specialty magazines related to personal investing that emphasize in-depth analysis of investment strategies. Topics covered include retirement planning, saving for college, and tax issues.

Investment Newsletters

Investment newsletters are double-edged swords. The investment advice given in newsletters is often wrong. At the same time, they can be a source of timely investment information. What concern us are the newsletters that claim to have a crystal ball. If any investment analyst really knew what the future held, why would they sell that information? They could make more money doing their own investing.

Clubs and Associations

Joining a stock investment club or even better, starting your own investment club, is one of the best ways to improve your investment skills and further your general education in personal investing. Investment clubs begin by club members providing "seed" money. Members hold regular meetings where they vote on investment decisions. Club associations also exist that provide various forms of information to their members. A well-known club association is the National Association of Investors Corporation (NAIC).

Mutual Fund Contact Information

Below is a list of mutual fund toll free numbers. Each of these companies has staff on hand to answer any questions you may have about investment choices they have available. Do not read this list as an endorsement.

Mutual Funds

Dreyfus	1-800-896-8172
Fidelity	1-800-544-6666
Franklin Templeton	1-800-372-6554
TIAA-CREF	1-800-842-1924
T. Rowe Price	1-800-541-2705
Vanguard	1-877-662-7447

21

+

How to Select
a Financial Planner

On your own, you can accomplish many of the tasks necessary to become financially secure. At the same time, most of you can't do everything. In personal investing, many complexities exist where a planner can help. For example, reducing the cost of your federal taxes. We believe that the more you know about personal investing, the more useful a planner becomes. Individuals new to financial planning often waste their planner's time and their own money by asking them questions that they can better answer on their own. Use a financial planner to answer difficult questions

One of the most important things about choosing a planner is your comfort level and trust the planner will provide you with sound advice that's in your best interest. If you're at that point where you believe a personal planner would be helpful, use the services of a certified financial planner (CFP). CFPs go through rigorous training and must pass an examination. Be wary of other professional headings.

A CFP can review and organize your entire financial picture. Areas covered include:

- Current and future income needs
- Financial goal setting (retirement planning, college savings)
- Insurance needs
- Net Worth Analysis
- Risk analysis
- Portfolio analysis

- Tax analysis
- Developing an *Action Plan*

Something to consider when selecting a planner is their method of compensation. Is their compensation fee- or commission-based?

A fee-based planner charges a flat rate per hour or a set dollar amount. A commission-based planner charges a fee based on a percentage of money managed or invested. Commission compensated planners may receive money from the mutual fund companies they recommend. This may affect their judgment. Ask your planner for a disclosure statement describing their affiliation(s) with investment companies and their method of payment.

22

Life Stage Concerns

AGES TWENTY TO THIRTY: STARTING OUT

Getting started with a career and establishing yourself can be scary. Most young Americans go through the following phases: get a job and begin a career, purchase a car, find a life partner and get married, buy a house, and start a family.

One commercial claims that "life comes at you fast," and we believe it. During your twenties, you'll be confronted with many life decisions and the choices you make will shape the rest of your personal and professional lives. We want you to make the right choices.

Start with good habits. This means setting career and financial goals, learning where you spend your money, living within your means, building a financial plan, and avoiding unnecessary debt. One of the most difficult things to do during your twenties is not spending every penny you earn. If you can begin to save between 10 and 20 percent of your gross income, then you'll be on your way to avoid future money problems.

Career Choice

Your career choice affects a lot of the analysis performed in previous chapters. Your first job's starting salary and its future salary projections determine how much you can spend and how much wealth you'll be able to accumulate. We believe you should choose a college major and a career that first maximizes your life satisfaction and not your pay. Almost regardless of your job and its pay, if you follow our book's advice you can build a financially secure life if you start young.

Building an Emergency Fund

Once you begin work, you must start to build an emergency fund. Follow our earlier advice on how much you need. Most Americans experience multiple job losses during their working lives. The purpose of this fund is to support you during unemployment.

Car

While you need a car, don't overspend when buying one. Cars depreciate and become worthless. Why do you want to put your hard-earned money into something that eventually will be worth nothing?

We recommend buying good used cars. When you buy a new car the moment you drive off the car dealer's lot, you lose thousands of dollars. Why would you do this when you have outstanding student loans and little wealth? Buy used cars, pay off your debt and begin saving and investing.

Student Loans

The average college student ends up with thousands of dollars of student loans. Check to see whether your loans are federal and/or private. Federal loans are student friendly. Beginning in 2014, new policies go into effect for federal loans. Check out their new rules. Upon graduation, consider consolidating your federal loans into a single payment. Make extra loan payments to your loans with the highest interest.

Retirement

When you're in your twenties retirement seems like it's a million years away. Well, it's not. Please don't tell yourself that you can't afford to begin saving for retirement. Engage in life cycle retirement saving. Even with all the other financial pressures you face, start to save something for retirement. Life cycle retirement saving means you increase the amount you save as you age and earn more income. Whatever you can afford to save toward retirement in your twenties, start doing it.

Marriage

One of the biggest mistakes couples make before marriage is not discussing the financial management of their union. It's not untypical among married couples for one partner to be a spender and the other a saver. This often leads to marital discord.

Before marriage, every couple needs to sit down and have an honest conversation about money. A couple has to work together on family finances. This means setting financial goals, creating a family budget, and setting ground rules on personal purchases. Both members in a marriage must be financially literate.

If you and your spouse work as a financial team, we promise you that only will you have a healthier and happier marriage but also a better sex life. Nothing spoils bedroom fun like fights over money.

Building a Credit History

When you're young it's important to start building up a history of borrowing money and paying it back on time. When a bill comes in the mail, open it and pay it. Bills left on the kitchen table have the habit of not being paid.

It's okay to use your credit cards and retail revolving debt to buy things if you're going to pay back the money you borrowed at the first billing cycle it's due. Don't use your credit card money or any form of retail debt as a long-term loan.

Make sure you pay all of your monthly bills. Don't hide from a bill you can't pay—believe us, it isn't going away. If you can't make a payment, call the lender and explain your situation. Often, lenders will work out some payment option for you.

The longer your credit history of paying bills on time the less risk you pose to lenders. The less risk you pose to lenders, the less interest they charge on borrowed money.

Saving for a Down Payment on a House

We hate to overload with things you need to do in your twenties but you should at least consider saving money for a house down payment. As of today, 20 percent down seems to be a reasonable number to save for. This means that if you want a $200,000 property you need to save $40,000—not a trivial sum. It's best to start accumulating this down payment money long before you need it.

AGES THIRTY TO FIFTY: FAMILY YEARS

These years are typically devoted to building a career and raising a family. Expenses are at their maximum. Children have a million ways of absorbing family resources. These are also the years of mortgage payments, high insurance costs, and saving for your children's college education and your retirement.

Buying a Home

For most people this is the single largest purchase they'll ever make. Make sure you buy a house you can afford. (Don't use your house to make a statement about your success.) This means mortgage payments affordable on a single salary and a fifteen-year mortgage. Pay off your house before you retire. If you buy a smaller house, then you'll also have lower utility bills and pay lower taxes. This will leave you more money for your emergency fund, retirement and saving for your children's college education.

Children

Most people know having children is expensive but still underestimate their true cost. Add up your additional housing, food, transportation, healthcare, childcare, and college cost because of children and you're easily over $250,000 per child. Most parents don't think about many of these added costs until it's too late.

College Funds

Our advice is simple when it comes to saving money for your children's college education: begin right now, if you haven't already started. The sooner you begin the easier it will be on your family's finances. Just $100 per month, earning 9 percent for eighteen years, will grow to over $50,000. Start saving the month your children are born and don't stop until they enter college. It's easier to find $100 a month now than the tens of thousands of dollars you'll need each year while they're in college.

Now for the opposite advice: don't sacrifice your retirement to pay for your children's education. If you can't fit college savings into your family's budget then don't do it. Let your children work and borrow money to pay for their own education.

Two ways of saving money on a college education are to attend a state school and to have your children attend a community college for their first two years of college. Community colleges are less expensive than four-year schools, and it's easy to transfer community college credit to a four-year state school.

Retirement and Emergency Funds

Once you have a family you must have an emergency fund. Depending on your situation, you need at least six month of "ready cash" to pay all of your family's bills if you lose your job.

The other thing you must do is start saving for your retirement. At the very least, maximize your company's match.

After these two goals are on track, then pursue a college fund.

Writing Your Will

Once you're married and have children you need a will. A will is not the place to determine your treatment during a medical crisis. This requires what's called a living will. A will has the following important parts:

Name an Executer

This is just naming a person who will carry out the instructions of your will. Typically, people name their spouse as the will's executor. It's important to also name an alternate executor should the first choice either not be available or unwilling to do it.

Name a Guardian for Minor Children

This is to provide a parent to your minor children if there is no remaining natural parent available. Whomever you select as guardian for your children, make sure they're willing to take on this role. If your choice involves a couple, make sure you state both their names in your will.

Name Beneficiaries

This is just explicitly providing the names of everyone who will receive the assets of your estate. Don't forget to include alternative beneficiaries in case of death.

Remember, it's very difficult to exclude a spouse from inheritance.

Specific Bequests

Bequests allow you to name persons and organizations that you want to receive specific property or cash sums.

Funeral Arrangements

Here you express your wishes on how your remains are to be disposed.

Your Signature

You must sign a will in the presence of witnesses. You need to also include a date and place of signing. It's recommended that you sign every page of the will.

Signature of Witnesses

Most states require the signatures of two witnesses of you signing your will. Witnesses must be adults of sound mind. Witnesses declare by their signatures that you're of sound mind and weren't under duress when you signed. Witnesses should not be will beneficiaries.

AGE FIFTY-PLUS: SUN AND FUN YEARS

Most individuals in this group find themselves taking a reflective look at their lives and ask, "where did the last thirty or so years go?" The older you become the faster time moves. Age fifty and above is when everyone gets serious about their future finances. If you were smart, you got serious about your finances when you graduated college.

Retirement

Now is the time you must ask yourself when you plan on retiring and how much monthly income you'll need. We hope that you asked this question earlier in your life and you've been saving and investing for retirement. Again, as we stated earlier, we're proponents of the 100 percent retirement income strategy. This way if you fall short of your goal then you'll probably have enough to live on anyway.

If you're going to be short retirement income, then you'll have to work longer or consider semiretirement. Most people who retire discover that their costs are much less than when they worked and raised a family. Children are now self-supporting, you don't have to save for retirement, many of your insurance costs are now less, work related expenses are mostly gone, you might be able to remove some of the equity in your house, and so on.

We suggest that you sit down with a certified financial planner or some other expert and carefully plot your future course. Calculate exactly what you'll need in retirement and whether you'll have sufficient assets to support yourself. Don't hide from this exercise. Even though it's late in the retirement game, you can still do things that make retirement a reality.

Long-term Care Insurance

The purpose of long-term care insurance is to pay the care costs of such devastating illnesses as Alzheimer's, stroke, and Parkinson's. It's now forecasted that over half of Americans will need long-term care. Long-term care costs now average $75,000 per year. Can you afford this type of money? If you're like the rest of us then probably not.

Long-term care insurance pays for assistance you need if your illness or disability makes you unable to care for yourself. It normally covers care provided in a nursing home, assisted living facility, or in your own home. While we mostly view long-term care as something the elderly might need, it also equally applies to younger or middle-aged people who have suffered some debilitating event.

What happens if you don't have long-term care insurance? How much can you rely on government help?

Medicare will pay for some portion of short-term skilled care needed following hospitalization. Medicare doesn't cover long-term care. Medigap and MedSupp cover some of the gaps in Medicare. If you meet federal poverty guidelines, Medicaid will pay a percentage of nursing home costs.

Two problems with relying on the public sector for long-term care are the quality of the care you receive and the need to rid yourself of assets to qualify for Medicaid. Relying on Medicaid to pay your nursing home costs will probably mean a lower quality nursing home. Some people give away their assets to their children to qualify for Medicaid. We see this as a second best strategy for covering your long-term care needs.

We suggest that you investigate the cost and need for long-term care with an insurance expert. Your family's health history and the insurance cost of long-term care have to be compared to make the right decision.

Grandchildren

Grandchildren are great. One way we suggest you can help them is to set up a college fund for them. Earlier we spoke about various college savings plans. Pick one that makes sense for you and begin saving for your grandchildren's education or contribute to the fund that their parents are using.

Also, consider starting a retirement fund for your grandchildren. Beginning a retirement fund at birth makes it easy to accumulate a million dollars by the time your grandkids are in their fifties.

Get the grandchildren's parents involved as well. One motivational tool is to offer a match for every dollar they invest in their children you'll also invest a certain percentage.

Estate Planning

Review the assets you want your heirs to inherit and whether this will require the assistance of an attorney who specializes in estate planning. The more complex the estate the more likely an attorney is necessary.

As part of the estate planning process, we encourage families to discuss exactly what you want done after you die. This includes funeral arrangements and everything else down to who gets individual pieces of jewelry. The more you plan and spell out your wishes the more likely they will be fulfilled.

You should also create a file that contains information about all investment accounts, insurance policies, and bank accounts along with all pertinent contact names and numbers. When you die, it's a very emotional time, and it will be much easier for your family to cope with their loss if they also don't have to go on a fishing expedition looking for your private financial information.

23

Summary of
Insights and Advice

FOURTEEN REASONS PEOPLE FAIL IN INVESTING

1. Procrastination
2. Lack of specific goals
3. Living beyond their means
4. Fear of the unknown
5. Buying stocks when their prices are too high
6. Miscalculating the amount of time and money needed to reach financial goals
7. Falling in love with an investment
8. Ignoring investment opportunities
9. Losing patience
10. Following a tip
11. Ignorance about taxes
12. Buying too much insurance
13. Lack of diversification
14. Lack of discipline

SUMMARY OF FACT

1. Over the long-term, among financial assets, stocks have the highest real return.
2. Stocks carry more risk than bonds and bonds carry more risk than cash assets.

3. Diversification reduces risk. To earn greater returns, you must expose yourself to greater risk.
4. Among financial assets, stocks are the best long-term hedge against inflation.
5. Rising interest rates depress returns on existing financial assets.
6. Historically, stocks with lower P/E ratios earn higher returns.
7. Historically, stocks with lower P/D ratios earn higher returns.

SOME OPTIONS TO HELP YOU MEET YOUR SAVINGS GOALS

1. Lengthen the time to reach your financial goals.
2. Eliminate or modify goals. You can't have everything.
3. Reduce your expenses. We never met a budget that couldn't be cut.
4. Increase your income. Working more, acquiring more education, and targeting a job promotion are various strategies you can use to boost your income.
5. Invest more aggressively. If you weigh your portfolio mix more towards stocks then you'll earn a higher portfolio rate of return. Of course, you're also taking on more risk.
6. Engage in life-cycle saving. In life-cycle saving it's expected that you'll save less when you are young and more as you become older and your income rises. Many families also cut back on their savings when their children are still in school and then boost savings when they become empty nesters.

Appendix 1

Future Value of Present Sum

	Rates	1%	2%	3%	4%	5%	6%	7%
Periods								
1		1.0100	1.0200	1.0300	1.0400	1.0500	1.0600	1.0700
2		1.0201	1.0404	1.0609	1.0816	1.1025	1.1236	1.1449
3		1.0303	1.0612	1.0927	1.1249	1.1576	1.1910	1.2250
4		1.0406	1.0824	1.1255	1.1699	1.2155	1.2625	1.3108
5		1.0510	1.1041	1.1593	1.2167	1.2763	1.3382	1.4026
6		1.0615	1.1262	1.1941	1.2653	1.3401	1.4185	1.5007
7		1.0721	1.1487	1.2299	1.3159	1.4071	1.5036	1.6058
8		1.0829	1.1717	1.2668	1.3686	1.4775	1.5938	1.7182
9		1.0937	1.1951	1.3048	1.4233	1.5513	1.6895	1.8385
10		1.1046	1.2190	1.3439	1.4802	1.6289	1.7908	1.9672
11		1.1157	1.2434	1.3842	1.5395	1.7103	1.8983	2.1049
12		1.1268	1.2682	1.4258	1.6010	1.7959	2.0122	2.2522
13		1.1381	1.2936	1.4685	1.6651	1.8856	2.1329	2.4098

Appendix 1

	Rates	1%	2%	3%	4%	5%	6%	7%
Periods								
14		1.1495	1.3195	1.5126	1.7317	1.9799	2.2609	2.5785
15		1.1610	1.3459	1.5580	1.8009	2.0789	2.3966	2.7590
16		1.1726	1.3728	1.6047	1.8730	2.1829	2.5404	2.9522
17		1.1843	1.4002	1.6528	1.9479	2.2920	2.6928	3.1588
18		1.1961	1.4282	1.7024	2.0258	2.4066	2.8543	3.3799
19		1.2081	1.4568	1.7535	2.1068	2.5270	3.0256	3.6165
20		1.2202	1.4859	1.8061	2.1911	2.6533	3.2071	3.8697
21		1.2324	1.5157	1.8603	2.2788	2.7860	3.3996	4.1406
22		1.2447	1.5460	1.9161	2.3699	2.9253	3.6035	4.4304
23		1.2572	1.5769	1.9736	2.4647	3.0715	3.8197	4.7405
24		1.2697	1.6084	2.0328	2.5633	3.2251	4.0489	5.0724
25		1.2824	1.6406	2.0938	2.6658	3.3864	4.2919	5.4274
26		1.2953	1.6734	2.1566	2.7725	3.5557	4.5494	5.8074

	Rates	1%	2%	3%	4%	5%	6%	7%
Periods								
27		1.3082	1.7069	2.2213	2.8834	3.7335	4.8223	6.2139
28		1.3213	1.7410	2.2879	2.9987	3.9201	5.1117	6.6488
29		1.3345	1.7758	2.3566	3.1187	4.1161	5.4184	7.1143
30		1.3478	1.8114	2.4273	3.2434	4.3219	5.7435	7.6123
31		1.3613	1.8476	2.5001	3.3731	4.5380	6.0881	8.1451
32		1.3749	1.8845	2.5751	3.5081	4.7649	6.4534	8.7153
33		1.3887	1.9222	2.6523	3.6484	5.0032	6.8406	9.3253
34		1.4026	1.9607	2.7319	3.7943	5.2533	7.2510	9.9781
35		1.4166	1.9999	2.8139	3.9461	5.5160	7.6861	10.6766
36		1.4308	2.0399	2.8983	4.1039	5.7918	8.1473	11.4239
37		1.4451	2.0807	2.9852	4.2681	6.0814	8.6361	12.2236
38		1.4595	2.1223	3.0748	4.4388	6.3855	9.1543	13.0793
39		1.4741	2.1647	3.1670	4.6164	6.7048	9.7035	13.9948

	Rates	1%	2%	3%	4%	5%	6%	7%
Periods								
40		1.4889	2.2080	3.2620	4.8010	7.0400	10.2857	14.9745
41		1.5038	2.2522	3.3599	4.9931	7.3920	10.9029	16.0227
42		1.5188	2.2972	3.4607	5.1928	7.7616	11.5570	17.1443
43		1.5340	2.3432	3.5645	5.4005	8.1497	12.2505	18.3444
44		1.5493	2.3901	3.6715	5.6165	8.5572	12.9855	19.6285
45		1.5648	2.4379	3.7816	5.8412	8.9850	13.7646	21.0025
46		1.5805	2.4866	3.8950	6.0748	9.4343	14.5905	22.4726
47		1.5963	2.5363	4.0119	6.3178	9.9060	15.4659	24.0457
48		1.6122	2.5871	4.1323	6.5705	10.4013	16.3939	25.7289
49		1.6283	2.6388	4.2562	6.8333	10.9213	17.3775	27.5299
50		1.6446	2.6916	4.3839	7.1067	11.4674	18.4302	29.4570

Rates		8%	9%	10%	11%	12%	13%	14%
Periods								
1		1.0800	1.0900	1.1000	1.1100	1.1200	1.1300	1.1400
2		1.1664	1.1881	1.2100	1.2321	1.2544	1.2769	1.2996
3		1.2597	1.2950	1.3310	1.3676	1.4049	1.4429	1.4815
4		4.3605	1.4116	1.4641	1.5181	1.5735	1.6305	1.6890
5		1.4693	1.5386	1.6105	1.6851	1.7623	1.8424	1.9254
6		1.5869	1.6771	1.7716	1.8704	1.9738	2.0820	2.1950
7		1.7138	1.8280	1.9487	2.0762	2.2107	2.3526	2.5023
8		1.8509	1.9926	2.1436	2.3045	2.4760	2.6584	2.8526
9		1.9990	2.1719	2.3579	2.5580	2.7731	3.0040	3.2519
10		2.1589	2.3674	2.5937	2.8394	3.1058	3.3946	3.7072
11		2.3316	2.5804	2.8531	3.1518	3.4786	3.8359	4.2263
12		2.5182	2.8127	3.1384	3.4985	3.8960	4.3345	4.8179
13		2.7396	3.0658	3.4523	3.8833	4.3635	4.8981	5.4924

	Rates	8%	9%	10%	11%	12%	13%	14%
Periods								
14		2.9372	3.3417	3.7975	4.3104	4.8871	5.5348	6.2613
15		3.1722	3.6425	4.1772	4.7846	5.4736	6.2543	7.1379
16		3.4259	3.9703	4.5950	5.3109	6.1304	7.0673	8.1372
17		3.7000	4.3276	5.0545	5.8951	6.8660	7.9861	9.2765
18		3.9960	4.7171	5.5599	6.5436	7.6900	9.0243	10.5752
19		4.3157	5.1417	6.1159	7.2633	8.6128	10.1974	12.0557
20		4.6610	5.6044	6.7275	8.0623	9.6463	11.5231	13.7435
21		5.0338	6.1088	7.4003	8.9492	10.8038	13.0211	15.6676
22		5.4365	6.6586	8.1403	9.9336	12.1003	14.7138	17.8610
23		5.8715	7.2579	8.9543	11.0263	13.5523	16.6266	20.3616
24		6.3412	7.9111	9.8497	12.2392	15.1786	18.7881	23.2122
25		6.8485	8.6231	10.8347	13.5855	17.0001	21.2305	26.4619
26		7.3964	9.3992	11.9182	15.0799	19.0401	23.9905	30.1666

	Rates	8%	9%	10%	11%	12%	13%	14%
Periods								
27		7.9881	10.2451	13.1100	16.7387	21.3249	27.1093	34.3899
28		8.6271	11.1671	14.4210	18.5799	23.8839	30.6335	39.2045
29		9.3173	12.1722	15.8631	20.6237	26.7499	34.6158	44.6931
30		10.0627	13.2677	17.4494	22.8923	29.9599	39.1159	50.9502
31		10.8677	14.4618	19.1943	25.4104	33.5551	44.2010	58.0832
32		11.7371	15.7633	21.1138	28.2056	37.5817	49.9471	66.21
33		12.6761	17.1820	23.2252	31.3082	42.0915	56.4402	75.4849
34		13.6901	18.7284	25.5477	34.7521	47.1425	63.7774	86.0528
35		14.7853	20.4140	28.1024	38.5749	52.7996	72.0685	98.1002
36		15.9682	22.2512	30.9128	42.8181	59.1356	81.4374	111.8342
37		17.2456	24.2538	34.0039	47.5281	66.2318	92.0243	127.4910
38		18.6253	26.4367	37.4043	52.7562	74.1797	103.9874	145.3397
39		20.1153	28.8160	41.1448	58.5593	83.0812	117.5058	165.6873

Appendix 1

	Rates	8%	9%	10%	11%	12%	13%	14%
Periods								
40		21.7245	31.4094	45.2593	65.0009	93.0510	132.7816	188.8835
41		23.4625	34.2363	49.7852	72.1510	104.2171	150.0432	215.3272
42		25.3395	37.3175	54.7637	80.0876	116.7231	169.5488	245.4730
43		27.3666	40.6761	60.2401	88.8972	130.7299	191.5901	279.8392
44		29.5560	44.3370	66.2641	98.6759	146.4175	216.4968	319.0167
45		31.9204	48.3273	72.8905	109.5302	163.9876	244.6414	363.6791
46		34.4741	52.6767	80.1795	121.5786	183.6661	276.4448	414.5941
47		37.2320	57.4176	88.1975	134.9522	205.7061	312.3826	472.6373
48		40.2106	62.5852	97.0172	149.7970	230.3908	352.9923	538.8065
49		43.4274	68.2179	106.7190	166.2746	258.0377	398.8814	614.2395
50		46.9016	74.3575	117.3909	184.5648	289.0022	450.7359	700.2330

Appendix 2

Future Value of Annuities

	Rates	1%	2%	3%	4%	5%	6%	7%
Periods								
1		1.0000	1.0000	1.0000	1.0000	1.0000	1.0000	1.0000
2		2.0100	2.0200	2.0300	2.0400	2.0500	2.0600	2.0700
3		3.0301	3.0604	3.0909	3.1216	3.1525	3.1836	3.2149
4		4.0604	4.1216	4.1836	4.2465	4.3101	4.3746	4.4399
5		5.1010	5.2040	5.3091	5.4163	5.5256	5.6371	5.7507
6		6.1520	6.3081	6.4684	6.6330	6.8019	6.9753	7.1533
7		7.2135	7.4343	7.6625	7.8983	8.1420	8.3938	8.6540
8		8.2857	8.5830	8.8923	9.2142	9.5491	9.8975	10.2598
9		9.3685	9.7546	10.1591	10.5828	11.0266	11.4913	11.9780
10		10.4622	10.9497	11.4639	12.0061	12.5779	13.1808	13.8164
11		11.5668	12.1687	12.8078	13.4864	14.2068	14.9716	15.7836
12		12.6825	13.4121	14.1920	15.0258	15.9171	16.8699	17.8885
13		13.8093	14.6803	15.6178	16.6268	17.7130	18.8821	20.1406

Appendix 2

	Rates	1%	2%	3%	4%	5%	6%	7%
Periods								
14		14.9474	15.9739	17.0863	18.2919	19.5980	21.0151	22.5505
15		16.0969	17.2934	18.5989	20.0236	21.5786	23.2760	25.1290
16		17.2579	18.6393	20.1569	21.8245	23.6575	25.6725	27.8881
17		18.4304	20.0121	21.7616	23.6975	25.8404	28.2129	30.8402
18		19.6147	21.4123	234144	25.6454	28.1324	30.9057	33.9990
19		20.8109	22.8406	25.1169	27.6712	30.5390	33.7600	37.3790
20		22.0190	24.2974	26.8704	29.7781	33.0660	36.7856	40.9955
21		23.2392	25.7833	28.6765	31.9692	35.7193	39.9927	44.8652
22		24.4716	27.2990	30.5368	34.2480	38.5052	43.3923	49.0057
23		25.7163	28.8450	32.4529	36.6179	41.4305	46.9958	53.4361
24		26.9735	30.4219	34.4265	39.0826	44.5020	50.8156	58.1767
25		28.2432	32.0303	36.4593	41.6459	47.7271	54.8645	63.2490
26		29.5256	33.6709	38.5530	44.3117	51.1135	59.1564	68.6765

	Rates	1%	2%	3%	4%	5%	6%	7%
Periods								
27		30.8209	35.3443	40.7096	47.0842	54.6691	63.7058	74.4838
28		32.1291	37.0512	42.9309	49.9676	58.4026	68.5281	80.6977
29		33.4504	38.7922	45.2189	52.9663	62.3227	73.6398	87.3465
30		34.7849	40.5681	47.5754	56.0849	66.4388	79.0582	94.4608
31		36.1327	42.3794	50.0027	59.3283	70.7608	84.8017	102.0730
32		37.4941	44.2270	52.5028	62.7015	75.2988	908898	110.2182
33		38.8690	46.1116	55.0778	66.2095	80.0638	97.3432	118.9334
34		40.2577	48.0338	57.7302	69.8579	85.0670	104.1838	128.2588
35		41.6603	49.9945	60.4621	73.6522	90.3203	111.4348	138.2369
36		43.0769	51.9949	63.2759	77.5983	95.8363	119.1209	148.9135
37		44.5076	54.0343	66.1742	81.7022	101.6281	127.2681	160.3374
38		45.9527	56.1149	69.1594	85.9703	107.7095	135.9042	172.5610
39		47.4123	58.2372	72.2342	90.4092	114.0950	145.0585	185.6403

Appendix 2

	Rates	1%	2%	3%	4%	5%	6%	7%
Periods								
40		48.8864	60.4020	75.4013	95.0255	120.7998	154.7620	199.6351
41		50.3752	62.6100	78.6633	99.8265	127.8398	165.0477	214.6096
42		51.8790	64.8622	82.0232	104.8196	135.2318	175.9505	230.6322
43		53.3978	67.1595	85.4839	110.0124	142.9933	187.5076	247.7765
44		54.9318	69.5027	89.0484	115.4129	151.1430	199.7580	266.1209
45		56.4811	71.8927	92.7199	121.0294	159.7002	212.7435	285.7493
46		58.0459	74.3306	96.5015	126.8706	168.6852	226.5081	306.7518
47		59.6263	76.8179	100.3965	132.9454	178.1194	241.0986	329.2244
48		61.2226	79.3535	104.4084	139.2632	188.0254	256.5645	353.2701
49		62.8348	81.9406	108.5406	145.8837	198.4267	272.9584	378.9990
50		64.4632	84.5794	112.7969	152.6671	209.3480	290.3359	406.5289

	Rates	8%	9%	10%	11%	12%	13%	14%
Periods								
1		1	1	1	1	1	1	1
2		2.08	2.09	2.1	2.11	2.12	2.13	2.14
3		3.2464	3.2781	3.31	3.3421	3.3744	3.4069	3.4396
4		4.5061	4.5731	4.5731	4.7097	4.7793	4.8497	4.9211
5		5.8666	5.9847	5.9847	6.2278	6.3528	6.4802	6.6101
6		7.3359	7.5233	7.5233	7.9128	8.1151	8.3227	8.5355
7		8.9228	9.2004	9.4872	9.7833	10.0890	10.4047	10.7305
8		10.6366	11.0285	11.4359	11.8594	12.2997	12.7573	13.2328
9		12.4876	13.0210	13.5795	14.1640	14.7757	15.4157	16.0853
10		14.4866	15.1929	15.9374	16.7220	17.5487	18.4197	19.3373
11		16.6455	17.5603	18.5312	19.5614	20.6546	21.8143	23.0445
12		18.9771	20.1407	21.3843	22.7132	24.1331	25.6502	27.2707
13		21.4953	22.9534	24.5227	26.2116	28.0291	29.9847	32.0887

Rates		8%	9%	10%	11%	12%	13%	14%
Periods								
14		24.2149	26.0192	27.9750	30.0949	32.3926	34.8827	37.5811
15		27.1521	29.3609	31.7725	34.4054	37.2797	40.4175	43.8424
16		30.3243	33.0034	35.9497	39.1899	42.7533	46.6717	50.9804
17		33.7502	36.9737	40.5447	44.5008	48.8837	53.7391	59.1176
18		37.4502	41.3013	45.5992	50.3959	55.7497	61.7251	68.3941
19		41.4463	46.0185	51.1591	56.9395	63.4397	70.7494	78.9692
20		45.7620	51.1601	57.2750	64.2028	72.0524	80.9468	91.0249
21		50.4229	56.7645	64.0025	72.2651	81.6987	92.4699	104.7684
22		55.4568	62.8733	71.4027	81.2143	92.5026	105.4910	120.4360
23		60.8933	69.5319	79.5430	91.1479	104.6029	120.2048	138.2970
24		66.7648	76.7898	88.4973	102.1742	118.1552	136.8315	158.6586
25		73.1059	84.7009	98.3471	114.4133	133.3339	155.6196	181.8708
26		79.9544	93.3240	109.1818	127.9988	150.3339	176.8501	208.3327

Rates	8%	9%	10%	11%	12%	13%	14%
Periods							
27	87.3508	102.7231	121.0999	143.0786	169.3740	200.8406	238.4993
28	95.3388	112.9682	134.2099	159.8173	190.6989	227.9499	272.8892
29	103.9659	124.1354	148.6309	178.3972	214.5828	258.5834	312.0937
30	113.2832	136.3075	164.4940	199.0209	241.3327	293.1992	356.7868
31	123.3459	149.5752	181.9434	221.9132	271.2926	332.3151	407.7370
32	134.2135	164.0370	201.1378	247.3236	304.8477	376.5161	465.8202
33	145.9506	179.8003	222.2515	275.5292	342.4294	426.4632	532.0350
34	158.6267	196.9823	245.4767	306.8374	384.5210	482.9034	607.5199
35	172.3168	215.7108	271.0244	341.5896	431.6635	546.6808	693.5727
36	187.1021	236.1247	299.1268	380.1644	484.4631	618.7493	791.6729
37	203.0703	258.3759	330.0395	422.9825	543.5987	700.1867	903.5071
38	220.3159	282.6298	364.0434	470.5106	609.8305	792.2110	1030.9981
39	238.9412	309.0665	401.4478	523.2667	684.0102	896.1984	1176.3378

	Rates	8%	9%	10%	11%	12%	13%	14%
Periods								
40		259.0565	337.8824	442.5926	581.8261	767.0914	1013.7042	1342.0251
41		280.7810	369.2919	487.8518	646.8269	860.1424	1146.4858	1530.9086
42		304.2435	403.5281	537.6370	718.9779	964.3595	1296.5289	1746.2358
43		329.5830	440.8457	592.4007	799.0655	1081.0826	1466.0777	1991.7088
44		356.9496	481.5218	652.6408	887.9627	1211.8125	1657.6678	2271.5481
45		386.5056	525.8587	718.9048	986.6386	1358.230	1874.164	2590.5648
46		418.4261	574.1860	791.7953	1096.168	1522.2176	2118.8060	2954.2439
47		452.9002	626.8628	871.9749	1217.7474	1705.8838	2395.2508	3368.8380
48		490.1322	684.2804	960.1723	1352.6996	1911.5898	2707.6334	3841.4753
49		530.3427	746.8656	1057.189	1502.4965	2141.9806	3060.6258	4380.2819
50		573.7702	815.0836	1163.908	1668.7712	2400.0182	3459.5071	4994.5213

Appendix 3

Federal Student Loan Options

Federal Student Loan Amounts and Terms for Loans Issued in 2013-14

This chart summarizes the interest rates, loan limits, and other terms for federal student loans issued from
July 1, 2013 through June 30, 2014.

Basic Eligibility Requirements		U.S. citizens or permanent residents, enrolled at least half time in a qualified program at a participating school, not in default on a prior federal student loan, and not previously convicted of a drug offense while receiving federal financial aid. Total aid, including student loans, cannot exceed the school's total cost of attendance (tuition and fees, room and board, transportation, personal and miscellaneous expenses). FAFSA required.
Stafford Loans	Types	**Subsidized Stafford Loan**: Available to undergraduate students on the basis of financial need. No credit check required. The federal government covers the interest on these loans while borrowers are enrolled at least half time. Interest is not charged until the student leaves school or is no longer enrolled at least half time. Monthly payments are not required until six months after leaving school.
		Unsubsidized Stafford Loan: Available to undergraduate and graduate students *regardless of financial need*. No credit check required. Interest is charged throughout the life of the loan. Monthly payments are not required until six months after leaving school.
	Annual Loan Limits	**Dependent undergraduates (most students under the age of 24)**: $5,500 as freshmen (including up to $3,500 subsidized); $6,500 as sophomores (including up to $4,500 subsidized); $7,500 as juniors and seniors (including up to $5,500 subsidized).
		Independent undergraduates (students age 24 or older) *and* **dependent students whose parents are unable to obtain PLUS Loans**: $9,500 as freshmen (including up to $3,500 subsidized); $10,500 as sophomores (including up to $4,500 subsidized); $12,500 as juniors and seniors (including up to $5,500 subsidized).
		Graduate students: $20,500 (or $40,500 for certain medical training).
	Aggregate Loan Limits	**Dependent students**: $31,000. **Independent undergraduates** *and* **dependent students whose parents are unable to obtain PLUS Loans**: $57,500. **Graduate and professional students**: $138,500 (or $224,000 for certain medical training) including undergraduate borrowing.
	Interest Rate	The interest rate for both **subsidized** and **unsubsidized** Stafford loans for undergraduates is 3.86%. The interest rate for unsubsidized Stafford loans made to graduate students is 5.41%. Rates are fixed for the life of the loan.
	Fee	1.051% if first disbursed before December 1, 2013; 1.072% if first disbursed on or after December 1, 2013.
	Eligibility Period for Subsidized Loans	New borrowers will not be eligible to receive additional subsidized Stafford loans after they have received those loans for a time period that is 150% of the published length of their program, and may also become responsible for interest that accrues on their loans after that time. Borrowers with any federal loans from before July 1, 2013 will not be affected.
PLUS Loans	Types	**Parent PLUS**: Loans to parents of dependent students to help pay for undergraduate education. Parents are responsible for all principal and interest.
		Grad PLUS: Additional loans to graduate and professional degree students to help cover education expenses.
	Additional Eligibility Requirements	Available regardless of financial need to parents of dependent students (Parent PLUS) and to graduate and professional students (Grad PLUS). Credit check required. The credit requirement can be met by a cosigner. May require a separate application in addition to the FAFSA.
	Loan Limit	Total cost of attendance minus other financial aid. No aggregate maximum.
	Interest Rate	6.41%
	Fee	4.204% if first disbursed before December 1, 2013; 4.288% if first disbursed on or after December 1, 2013.
During Repayment	Rate reduction for automatic electronic payments	0.25% interest rate reduction.
	Unemployment deferment or economic hardship	May defer payments for up to three years. For Parent PLUS, Grad PLUS, and unsubsidized Stafford Loans, interest continues to accrue.
	Income-Driven Repayment Plans	There are three income-driven repayment plans that can help keep payments manageable for borrowers with relatively high debt compared to their income: Income-Based Repayment (IBR), Pay As You Earn, and Income Contingent Repayment (ICR). For more information about these plans, see studentaid.ed.gov and www.IBRinfo.org.
	Loan Forgiveness	Public Service Loan Forgiveness is available after 10 years of qualifying payments and employment, only for Direct Loans (excluding Parent PLUS). Teacher loan forgiveness programs (Stafford only) are available for loans in both the Direct and FFEL programs. All federal loans issued since July 1, 2010 are direct loans.
	Variable-Rate Loans	All Stafford and PLUS loans originated since July 1, 2006 have fixed rates. For older Stafford and PLUS loans with variable rates, interest rates change annually on July 1, based on the last 91-day T-bill auction in May.

For more information about federal student aid, please visit the Department of Education's http://studentaid.ed.gov.

Appendix 4

Answers to Equations

1. $2500 × 21.7245 = $54,311.25

    If you make a single investment of $2500 for forty years at 8 percent then you'll have $54,311.25.

2. $10,00 × 2.4066 = $24,066

    If you make a single investment of $10,000 for eighteen years at 5 percent then you'll have $24,066.

3. $2500 × 5.4163 = $13,540.75

    If you invest $2500 a year for five years and you earn 4 percent return each year then you'll have $13,540.75.

4. $5,000 × 406.5289 = $2,032,644.5

    If you invest $5,000 a year for fifty years and you earn 7 percent return each year then you'll have $2,032,644.5.

About the Authors

Mark A. Nadler, PhD, is A. L. Garber Family of Economics at Ashland University and department chair of economics and finance in the Dauch School of Business and Economics. He is the author of numerous publications in economic education and personal finance and is a co-founder of The Financial Education Company, LLC. In the past, Mark served as a columnist for Employee Benefit News in the area of financial education.

Terry E. Rumker, CFP® is a professor of finance and assistant director of the Institute for Contemporary Financial Studies in the Dauch College of Business and Economics at Ashland University. He is president and owner of Rumker Financial Services and co-founder of The Financial Education Company, LLC. Over the last twenty years, Terry has worked with individuals and Fortune 500 company employees in the area of financial planning.